24 EXCITING PLAYS
FOR
ANCIENT HISTORY
CLASSES

DEAN R. BOWMAN

J. WESTON
WALCH
PUBLISHER

PORTLAND, MAINE

User's Guide
to
Walch Reproducible Books

As part of our general effort to provide educational materials which are as practical and economical as possible, we have designated this publication a "reproducible book." The designation means that purchase of the book includes purchase of the right to limited reproduction of all pages on which this symbol appears:

Here is the basic Walch policy: We grant to individual purchasers of this book the right to make sufficient copies of reproducible pages for use by all students of a single teacher. This permission is limited to a single teacher, and does not apply to entire schools or school systems, so institutions purchasing the book should pass the permission on to a single teacher. Copying of the book or its parts for resale is prohibited.

Any questions regarding this policy or requests to purchase further reproduction rights should be addressed to:

Permissions Editor
J. Weston Walch, Publisher
321 Valley Street • P. O. Box 658
Portland, Maine 04104-0658

Cover art adapted from a sarcophagus relief, Ptolemaic period.

1   2   3   4   5   6   7   8   9   10
ISBN 0-8251-2098-5

Contents

To the Teacher v

The Plays

To the Teacher

These 24 plays were written to involve students in the "drama" of ancient history. They are not meant to replicate the dialogue of historical persons. Rather, these plays, set in various historical epochs, reflect what characters from ancient history *might* have said. While some of the plays may seem more mythological than factually historical, they are based on literature of the period and do reflect the concerns and attitudes of the time. As the teacher you can choose whether or not to use certain plays, or to use them to prompt a discussion of the difference between history and myth. While the plays may be produced for an audience, they are designed primarily for reading. Each reading should take between 10 and 15 minutes. The following suggestions may help you incorporate these plays into your ancient-history curriculum.

1. Use the plays during the middle or end of the unit.

2. Run off one complete copy of the appropriate play for each student in your class, plus 10 (for future reserves). If possible, make two-sided copies to save paper. Alternatively, copy different plays on different-colored paper, so you can quickly tell if all your students are reading the right pages.

3. Assign roles as homework to a selected group. Tell this group that you expect their best possible oral reading. (Otherwise the reading can be dull.)

4. Have the nonparticipants silently read along, and assign them the task of writing down two new things they learned from the work. Also, remind them that their time to read will come.

5. If the play is to be produced, have students research period costumes and scenery. You and your students may decide as a group what works best concerning character entrances, exits, and positioning.

6. Have students write their own historical plays! Emphasize the need for comprehensive research and the necessity of choosing characters and scenes that elicit substantive dialogue.

Problems of Early Peoples

Characters

SAGESSE, a wise man
LORO, his parrot
SKICK and DUG,
    Sagesse's aides

FANE and ORMILIG,
    wanderers

Scene I: Under a large tree, somewhere in the Eastern Hemisphere, a long, long time ago.

SAGESSE: Loro, look. Two visitors approach. Call Skick and Dug.

LORO: (*whistles*) Skick! Dug! We've got company. Real strange ones. Get your Polaroids ready.

SKICK: You called, oh Wise One?

SAGESSE: Yes. Please make our visitors feel welcome.

DUG: I don't think they can speak.

LORO: They're nothing but savages. Look how they pull their scraggly hair.

SKICK: What painful facial expressions they make.

DUG: What can this behavior mean?

SAGESSE: Chronic depression from miserable life-styles.

LORO: Send them both to psychiatrists.

SKICK:	How absurd! Who could understand them?
SAGESSE:	Good point, Skick. What they need is language.
LORO:	And some strong deodorant and mouthwash!
DUG:	Shut up, feather-head!
SAGESSE:	Skick, Dug, accompany these two to my vacation condo. Return when they have learned language.
SKICK:	Written, too?
SAGESSE:	Of course. They'll need to take notes.

Scene II: A few months later.

LORO:	(*whistles*) The hairy ones are back. Hope they both had good long baths.
DUG:	Wise One, allow me to introduce Fane and Ormilig.
SAGESSE:	Welcome. Now, what have you learned about them?
DUG:	You were right. Both of them were very depressed. They left their people to find a better life.
SAGESSE:	Be specific. What problems did they have?
SKICK:	We've taught them much, and now they can speak for themselves.
FANE:	Oh, Wise One, our lives were so hard.
ORMILIG:	And *boring!*
SAGESSE:	Tell us more.
FANE:	The same food, raw and stringy meat, day after day after day . . . .

24 Exciting Plays for Ancient History Classes

ORMILIG:	And no safe and comfortable places to rest.
LORO:	No problem. There's a Taco Bell next to a Motel 6 just beyond the sunset.
SKICK:	Loro, ever heard of parrot soup?
SAGESSE:	That's enough. We're here to solve problems, not create them. Now, think . . . . What could these people use?
DUG:	A . . . a . . . . Fire!
SKICK:	Makes the meat taste better, and keeps you warm. Plus, it scares away dangerous animals.
SAGESSE:	Anything else? Wild game isn't always available.
DUG:	A . . . a . . . . Berries! And other wild plants.
SAGESSE:	Yes, but what can you do when you've picked them bare?
SKICK:	Farming! Agriculture! We'll teach Fane and Ormilig all about planting and harvesting grain.
DUG:	Of course . . . . And how to grind it into flour for making bread.
LORO:	Yeah, and how to deep-fry it for doughnuts.
FANE:	Sounds great. But there's more to life than eating.
ORMILIG:	Right. We're tired of wearing these animal skins. They're hard to fit.
FANE:	Yeah. And they're too stiff and hard.
LORO:	Give them a Land's End catalog. They have some very stylish jackets.

24 Exciting Plays for Ancient History Classes

SKICK: How about a parrot-feather suit?

SAGESSE: We can help in this matter, too. Dug can teach you all about sheep and their wool.

DUG: Certainly. But first I have to show them how to make sharp tools to shear off the wool. You get some copper and tin. Then you heat them together to make bronze . . . .

LORO: Going to the nearest hardware store would be much easier.

SKICK: And that's only a few thousand years away!

SAGESSE: How about planting cotton? After all, it "breathes." Skick, you can teach them.

SKICK: I suppose, but I hate all those seeds—takes forever to comb them out.

LORO: Call my friend Eli. It's long distance, but I know he can solve your seed problem.

ORMILIG: We need help moving things . . . large, heavy things . . . and lots of little things at one time. A person's only got two hands, and my feet and back sure get tired.

SAGESSE: Dug, you're the mechanical one.

DUG: Very simple. We make a cart and hook it to a strong, tame animal like a horse or ox. But first we have to make some wheels.

LORO: Be sure to make them round this time.

DUG: Loro, I'm going to make your neck one of the spokes if you don't knock off the wisecracks.

SAGESSE: These projects should keep you all very busy for some time.

FANE:	Very true, and we're grateful for all your help. But as I previously stated, there's more to life than—
SAGESSE:	The basic necessities of food, shelter, and clothing. Skick, you're the artistic one . . . .
SKICK:	Thank you. Fane, Ormilig, I'll teach you how to express and communicate your deepest thoughts and feelings, how to entertain yourself and others.
ORMILIG:	That would be great. Our only diversion is throwing rocks and sticks at each other. And they can hurt.
LORO:	You need hockey helmets. How about baseball? Tennis, anyone?
SKICK:	I'll teach you painting, music, dance, drama . . . .
SAGESSE:	In time . . . . I think you're both ready to return to your people. Skick and Dug will accompany you and teach you these things where you live.
FANE:	We would like that, but they cannot come with us. Our people would do them great harm.
SAGESSE:	Why? Have they no laws? No peaceful order?
ORMILIG:	None. It's every person for himself or herself. The strongest rule. Only those who submit survive.
FANE:	That's another reason why we left.
SAGESSE:	You and your people need justice and protection. That's what laws and government are for.
LORO:	But watch out for politicians.
ORMILIG:	What's that bird talking about?

SAGESSE: Oh, something that always seems to be put in civilization's bag. Upon further reflection, I think you need to spend a little more time here.

LORO: Yeah, so you can learn how to cope with marriage problems by watching *Divorce Court.*

DUG: Loro! That's enough! No potato chips for a week!

Life in Ancient Sumer
(A Boy's "Education")

Characters

HOADI, a mother   **AROEL,** a father and scribe
LANI, a girl   **NARAM,** a foreman on a farm
ZEF, a boy

Scene I: Early morning, Ur, Sumer, c. 3000 B.C.

HOADI: Zef . . . . Zef! Time to get up! You don't want to be late for school again! Zef! Lani, be a good girl and wake up your lazy brother.

LANI: Zef! Wake up or I'll water the hair on your empty head!

ZEF: Leave me alone! I'll box your ears if you don't get out of here!

LANI: Touchy, touchy, big brother. Mother, Zef refuses to move. What should I do?

HOADI: Go and get your father.

AROEL: Here I am. Zef, if you're not at the table in sixty seconds, I'll put you on a trading boat where you'll row like a naked slave the rest of your life!

ZEF: I'm up!

HOADI: The master teacher said if you're late once more, he'll remove you from the school.

AROEL: Son, don't throw away your whole future.

LANI:	I wish I could go to school like Zef.
HOADI:	Hush, now, Lani. You know only boys can attend scribes' school.
LANI:	Zef's so lucky. It's not fair!
ZEF:	Won't you people listen to me for a change? I hate that school! I hate it! I hate it!
HOADI:	Shame on you! How could you say such a thing? Don't you realize what your father had to do to get you enrolled?
ZEF:	I don't care! I still hate it!
HOADI:	Do you have any idea how disappointed this makes us feel? Don't you care about our feelings?
ZEF:	How about mine? You don't know how horrible that school is. From sunup to sundown, doing nothing but sitting on a hard bench trying to learn two thousand stupid writing characters.
HOADI:	Did you think becoming a scribe would be easy?
LANI:	Nothing good is ever accomplished without hard work, sweat, and some pain.
ZEF:	Does that mean getting beaten for not knowing your lessons perfectly? I've had enough of that. I'm quitting.
HOADI:	How ridiculous! You're throwing away the chance to have one of the best jobs in all Sumer.
LANI:	Let me take Zef's place. I know just as much cuneiform as he does.
ZEF:	Dad, just face it. I'm not cut out to be a scribe. I don't care about the good pay or high prestige.

HOADI:	This is the worst tragedy our family has ever had to endure. How have I failed as a mother?
AROEL:	Calm down, now. I'm going to take the day off and see what other jobs might interest our son.
HOADI:	Where are you going?
AROEL:	All over town and into the countryside.
LANI:	I want to go! I want to go! Please take me, too!
HOADI:	No! I need you here.

Scene II: Farming area, later that day.

AROEL:	So you don't want to work in the court system?
ZEF:	Not there. They didn't argue and fight. The court guy tried to get everybody to agree.
AROEL:	It's called arbitration, and that "guy" was the public arbitrator. His job is to find a fair settlement both sides can agree to. We don't like bringing in the law, except as a last resort.
ZEF:	I'd rather be outside moving around, anyway.
	(They come upon NARAM.)
AROEL:	Naram, old friend, could you please show my son around— and put him to work for a few hours?
NARAM:	With pleasure.
AROEL:	Zef, without our fertile soil and efficient irrigation system, our city, as we know it, would not exist.
ZEF:	What do you mean?

AROEL:	We produce food very efficiently. Half the population can produce enough food to feed all the people. This enables the other half to pursue tasks besides farming . . .
NARAM:	Such as construction, handcrafts, trade, finance, education . . . . Are you ready to work?
ZEF:	Yes. I think I'm going to like this. Anything will be better than school.

Scene III: NARAM's farm, a few hours later.

AROEL:	Well, Son, how was it?
ZEF:	I want to go home. I'm hungry, all my muscles ache, and my hands feel as if they've held hot coals for a whole minute.
AROEL:	Those *are* nasty blisters. What did you do?
ZEF:	Helped dig a new irrigation channel.
AROEL:	Very important work! Without those channels we can't control flooding or conserve water for irrigation in the dry months.
ZEF:	Yeah, yeah. Naram told me all about it. It's too hard, though. I'm starved. Please take me to the market.
AROEL:	Do you have anything to barter for food?
ZEF:	Of course not. Come on, Dad. You must have some money.
AROEL:	Where would I get that?
ZEF:	Dad, Dad. Don't play dumb. You have a good, steady job that I know pays very well.
AROEL:	How do you know that, Zef?

ZEF:	Just look at our house. It has two stories. These farmers live in simple reed huts covered with dried mud. Mom has lots of jewelry and pottery. We all have expensive leather sandals.
AROEL:	Right. Now, don't you play dumb with me. What's my job?
ZEF:	You're a scribe.
AROEL:	Brilliant! Now, did I become one by eating some magical food, or by wishing real hard, or by making a special sacrifice at the ziggurat?
ZEF:	I see where you're leading. You win.
AROEL:	The game's not over yet. Do you realize how important writing is to our civilization? Without it, none of our complex business transactions would be possible—trading contracts, inventory and record keeping, property measurement and ownership deeds.
ZEF:	I see.
AROEL:	Without writing there'd be chaos. We'd all be back to hunting and gathering. Ready to go back to school?
ZEF:	Yeah. But can we get something to eat first?
AROEL:	Why not? I have a few silver coins. Let's jog to the nearest fruit stand.
ZEF:	Uh, Dad . . . . One more thing. My legs are killing me. Do you think we could—
AROEL:	Hire a donkey cart? Why not? Isn't that why we Sumerians invented the wheel? But no more special requests. And when we get home be sure to tell your mother all you've learned today.
ZEF:	Yeah, yeah.

Egypt, 2500 B.C.

Characters

MENDO, a Phoenician
merchant
HAK and SHULG,
Mendo's aides

FAHD and RAHN, Egyptian
merchant seamen
LANAH, wife of chief
minister's assistant

Scene I: Byblos, ancient Syria, June, 2500 B.C.

MENDO:	Hak, Shulg, here's your ship.
HAK:	It's beautiful!
MENDO:	The Egyptians take great pride in their sailing vessels. That's why they buy only the finest timbers—ours.
SHULG:	Cedars of Lebanon. They sure come a long way for wood. Why don't they use their own?
MENDO:	Egypt doesn't grow any . . . only papyrus.
HAK:	What's pa . . . pap . . . .
MENDO:	Papyrus. You'll find out all about it once you dock in Egypt. It's very important to their whole way of life. Hey, you two better get on board.
SHULG:	Anything else, Boss?
MENDO:	Yes, indeed. The Egyptians are my best customers. Find out where and how they might use more of our lumber. Observe how they keep such accurate and tidy business records. Visit their workshops and watch their craftsmen at work. Remember, it's their finished goods we barter our timbers for.

HAK:	We'll be all eyes and ears. See you in a year.

Scene II: Aboard ship, Nile delta, Lower Egypt, July.

SHULG:	Fahd, what is this?
FAHD:	The Nile, Mother of Egypt.
HAK:	*The* Nile? But it doesn't look like a river. It's—it's so wide.
FAHD:	This time of year the Nile rises and floods its banks. Here, at its entrance to the Mediterranean, the whole broad plain becomes like a sea.
SHULG:	Why do you call it "Mother of Egypt"?
FAHD:	The Nile is the source of our life.
HAK:	Because it brings us fresh water, right?
FAHD:	Yes . . . . But it brings us more than just water.
RAHN:	As we journey upstream you'll see what else.

Scene III: A day later, still on board.

FAHD:	Hak, Shulg, look to the east, and then to the west. What do you see?
SHULG:	Near the water's edge, rows of simple mud houses.
RAHN:	And beyond them?
HAK:	Desert—only dry, brown desert.

FAHD: Precisely. In a hundred days or so the Nile will recede, leaving behind rich, black soil. As soon as possible the farmers will plow and plant.

RAHN: And a green carpet of crops will soon spring up on the river's edge.

FAHD: By March the grain will be harvested.

RAHN: And the Pharaoh's tax men will descend!

SHULG: You mean every year, year in and year out, the Nile refreshes the growing fields?

FAHD: Yes. But sometimes it rises too high.

RAHN: Or not high enough.

HAK: What then? Certain disaster, I would think.

FAHD: Not necessarily. Look more closely, near the houses.

SHULG: Are those little streams? I don't understand.

RAHN: They're canals we've built. They help control flooding.

FAHD: And enable us to irrigate our many fields.

RAHN: You must understand that here in Egypt we receive virtually no rainfall.

FAHD: Only the Nile gives us water. We collect and store it in large cisterns.

RAHN: For over seven hundred miles this system of canals and cisterns extends up the Nile. It's the foundation of Egypt's great civilization.

HAK: Incredible! But how did you put it all together?

FAHD: By a completely cooperative effort. Only when the people were mobilized for this massive project could the Nile's riches be tapped.

RAHN: And that mobilization required a strong central political authority—our Pharaoh and his bureaucracy.

FAHD: Our Pharaoh unites us, and that is Egypt's strength.

SHULG: But with all your wealth, why haven't you been invaded?

RAHN: Did you forget what was beyond our villages?

SHULG: Desert.

FAHD: To the east and west, farther than one can see. They are our guarding walls.

HAK: What about invasion from the sea?

RAHN: Our ships are too strong and numerous.

FAHD: And no one knows the Nile like we Egyptians.

RAHN: We're constantly using it for commerce and communication.

FAHD: And the two different currents make it easy to use.

SHULG: What? You've lost me now.

RAHN: The Nile's current flows from south to north.

SHULG: But we're sailing from north to south.

FAHD: Very perceptive! We're sailing now, not drifting as we'll do on the return trip. Along the Nile, the winds generally blow from north to south.

HAK: So the Nile works for you both ways. You Egyptians are very fortunate, except for this blasted heat! How can you take it every day?

| RAHN: | Be patient. You'll soon see how we've accommodated ourselves to the sun. |

Scene IV: Near Gizeh, on the Nile, a few days later.

| FAHD: | Hak, Shulg, wake up! We have something very special to show you. Just look over there. |

| SHULG: | What's that? . . . I must be still dreaming. |

| RAHN: | You're very much awake. That's a pyramid. Its construction is nearly complete. |

| SHULG: | But the size! It's like a mountain! That's it, then . . . . It's just a mountain you scraped and shaped. |

| FAHD: | No, my friend. If we were closer you'd see it's made of thousands of limestone blocks. |

| RAHN: | Each weighing up to fifteen tons. |

| HAK: | Preposterous! How could you possibly raise such immense objects so high? |

| FAHD: | With an ever-rising ramp. Along this incline plane the men use rollers and sledges to move the great blocks. |

| RAHN: | The apex of this pyramid is over four hundred and eighty feet high. |

| HAK: | Simply amazing! But tell me, who are the manual workers? Surely they must be slaves. |

| FAHD: | The work is indeed difficult. But these men are not slaves. They are free citizens who have time for this work during the flooding season. |

RAHN:	They're given plenty of bread and beer for their efforts.
FAHD:	That's an Egyptian's staple diet.
SHULG:	But what function can pyramids possibly serve? Certainly not a military one.
FAHD:	Correct. Deep inside, our king, the Pharaoh, will one day be buried.
HAK:	What? You must be joking. That gigantic edifice all for one man's bones?
RAHN:	Try to understand. . . . We believe our Pharaoh is descended from the gods; he is our link to them.
SHULG:	Housing a *living* king in a palace I can understand. But a corpse? Incomprehensible!
FAHD:	In our religion, death is simply a continuation of this life.
HAK:	So a pyramid is a palace for the next life?
RAHN:	For foreigners, that's sufficient understanding.
FAHD:	Look ahead. We'll soon be landing.
HAK:	Good. We're anxious to see how your people live in *this* life.

Scene V: Boat landing, near Memphis.

FAHD:	Alert the crew for docking.
SHULG:	What's that tall grass near the bank?
RAHN:	Another gift from our mother, the Nile.
SHULG:	What? It looks like a nuisance.

24 Exciting Plays for Ancient History Classes

FAHD: It's just the opposite. We call it "papyrus" and use it for more things than you can count.

HAK: Such as?

FAHD: Mats, baskets, furniture, sandals, roofs, and light boats.

HAK: Amazing. It looks as if you have an endless supply.

RAHN: Fahd, you forgot to mention writing.

SHULG: You don't use clay tablets?

FAHD: Too cumbersome. The scrolls we make from papyrus are thin, durable, and easy to store. They're ideal for lengthy record keeping.

RAHN: And we also use the papyrus growths as hunting grounds.

FAHD: Nobles love to hunt there. They use special sticks—

RAHN: And trained cats to retrieve the game.

HAK: Now you're really putting us on.

FAHD: Not in the least. It's been a long trip, and now it's time you two enjoyed a real Egyptian party.

Scene VI: Noble's house, Memphis, a short time later.

RAHN: This is the home of the chief minister's assistant.

LANAH: Welcome, visitors from the East. Are you hungry?

HAK: Why, yes. Thank you.

FAHD: You won't get peasant bread and beer here.

LANAH:	Please sit down. My servants will attend to your desires.
SHULG:	Thank you, again. Fahd, Rahn, please tell us what we're about to eat.
RAHN:	This platter contains leeks, beans, radishes, cucumbers, lettuce . . . and some honey to sweeten your palate.
FAHD:	And that one contains meat: beef, sheep, and goat. Also some fowl. Wine or beer?
HAK:	What a feast! So delicious! But tell me about the other guests. Is that their real hair? And what's that on their skin?
RAHN:	To protect our skin from the sun, we apply special oils. We also use many cosmetics, like eye liner.
FAHD:	As for their hair . . . . Those are wigs, with perfumed cones on top. They're worn for festive occasions like this.
SHULG:	It certainly is festive! Delicious food, pleasant aromas, music, dancing, smiling faces . . . .
RAHN:	We Egyptians like to enjoy life, and not just in the future.
FAHD:	And we'll continue to do so, as long as we remain united.
HAK:	Unity. I'll drink to that! And thanks!

Abraham: Monotheism
and the Covenant

Scene I: Ur in Chaldea, c. 2100 B.C.

YEDI: Who calls at the house of Terah?

ZOG: Zog, chief of the temple guards. I wish to speak with your master. The matter is most urgent.

YEDI: I'll get him at once.

TERAH: What's wrong? I adhere to all temple rules.

ZOG: You do, but not your son, Abram.

TERAH: He has a mind of his own. He's always talking about the one true God.

ZOG: He does more than talk! In the temple today he overturned more than half the idols before we stopped him!

TERAH: I'm sorry. But you know how impulsive and rebellious youth can be.

ZOG: Of course . . . . But as the guards were restraining him, he began preaching to the gathering crowd, calling them all idolators and fools.

TERAH:	Where is he now?
ZOG:	Nearby with my assistants.
TERAH:	Is he under arrest? Will he be tried and jailed?
ZOG:	Only if you don't cooperate. The chief priest wants to quietly end this unsettling affair. You and your household must leave Ur immediately.
TERAH:	What? Leave my house and business? Leave Ur? Where would I go?
ZOG:	Where you go is your affair. But leave you must. We cannot remain a great city when people like your son seek to undermine its foundation. He even told the crowd it was wrong to bring sacrifices to our temple, especially prisoners of war.
TERAH:	Very well, then . . . . Good-bye, Ur, and all your glory and grandeur, your bustling market and magnificent temples, your life-giving canals and matchless schools. For what? To roam into the unknown, where famine and danger always lurk. All because of my son, the dreamer, and his one, and only one, God.

Scene II: Haran, many years later.

SARAH:	Abram, my husband, what troubles your sleep?
ABRAHAM:	Visions and voices.
SARAH:	What do they concern?
ABRAHAM:	The Lord has promised a new land for our people—Canaan to the south.
SARAH:	Are we to leave Haran? The land is good and fertile.
ABRAHAM:	The Lord has spoken.

24 Exciting Plays for Ancient History Classes

SARAH: Ask your nephew, Lot, what he thinks. I fear we'll only meet with distress and death if we leave our homes here.

ABRAHAM: The Lord has spoken! Help ready the caravan.

Scene III: Bethel, years later.

LOYA: Abram, there have been harsh words, even fighting, between our shepherds and Lot's.

ABRAHAM: Why? Aren't we one people?

LOYA: Yes. But there are too many people and too many flocks for this one place.

ABRAHAM: *(walking toward LOT)* I will go to my nephew . . . .

LOT: You look troubled, dear Uncle.

ABRAHAM: Remember long ago why we did not stay here?

LOT: There was famine, so you led us to Egypt. Now we are both very prosperous.

ABRAHAM: Indeed, the Lord has blessed us both. But our servants quarrel and fight. We must divide the land. Look about and choose. I only want peace and harmony between our households.

LOT: You are very generous. The plain of the Jordan River will be our new home.

ABRAHAM: A fertile land with many rich cities. Go in peace, dear Nephew.

Scene IV: Canaan, many years later.

SARAH: Abram, do you feel bitter?

ABRAHAM: Because Lot left us and now lives in a very wicked city?

© 1992 J. Weston Walch, Publisher

24 Exciting Plays for Ancient History Classes

SARAH: No, no . . . . Because I am barren. Who will lead our people when you are gone? Take my maidservant, Hagar, so your seed will not die.

Scene V: Canaan, many years later.

SARAH: Your son grows in health and strength. I'm certain he'll become a great leader.

ABRAHAM: But not of our people. Ishmael has another destiny.

SARAH: What do you mean? I thought that's why . . . .

ABRAHAM: The Lord has spoken to me. Sarai, you will bear our son.

SARAH: Ha! You and the Lord make fun of me. I'm an old woman!

ABRAHAM: I laughed as well. Our son will be called *Isaac.*

SARAH: Our word for laughter.

ABRAHAM: And our names are to be Abraham and Sarah. Circumcision will be the sign of the Covenant.

Scene VI: ABRAHAM's tent, some time later.

SARAH: What's that horrible stench?

ABRAHAM: Rest here . . . . I'll go out and see.

SARAH: Is there a fire?

ABRAHAM: It's all over. Only the smoke lingers.

SARAH: What's all over?

ABRAHAM: The cities of the plain. Sodom and Gomorrah are no more. The Lord told me He would destroy them because of their wickedness.

SARAH: But Lot was a good man who honored the Lord God.

(Enter NOLAR, a messenger.)

NOLAR: Is Abraham here? I have urgent news.

ABRAHAM: I am Abraham.

NOLAR: Your nephew and his daughters escaped the great destruction.

ABRAHAM: What about Lot's wife?

NOLAR: At first she, too, was spared. But she disobeyed the Lord and looked back upon Sodom's fires.

SARAH: Out with it! What happened to her?

NOLAR: Her . . . her body became a pillar of salt.

ABRAHAM: We must leave this place.

Scene VII: Kingdom of Abimelech, years later.

SARAH: Abraham, do you ever think about Ishmael?

ABRAHAM: Why do you ask?

SARAH: I worry that you resent me for begging you to send Ishmael and Hagar away.

ABRAHAM: I don't resent you. The Lord ordered me. I must obey the Lord God, even when He asks me to do very difficult things.

SARAH:	Look at your eyes! You can't hide your tears for Ishmael.
ABRAHAM:	The Lord promised him a great destiny . . . . I weep for our dear son.
SARAH:	Isaac? What now does the Lord demand?
	(Enter FENDAL and SIGEN, two servants.)
FENDAL:	All is ready. Isaac waits.
SARAH:	Where are you going? What are you going to do?
ABRAHAM:	I'm going to Moriah, to place a burnt offering before the Lord.

Scene VIII: Region of Moriah, three days later.

ABRAHAM:	You two remain here with the donkey. Isaac and I will return after we worship.
	(ABRAHAM and ISAAC exit.)
SIGEN:	Isaac carries the wood. His father, the fire and knife.
FENDAL:	But . . . but there's no lamb. What is to be the sacrifice?
SIGEN:	Dare we follow them?
	(They follow furtively.)
FENDAL:	Abraham has bound Isaac on the altar!
SIGEN:	Oh, no! He's raising his knife! Why?
FENDAL:	I can't stand to look! This is too awful!

SIGEN:	Wait! His knife hand is stilled! Now he's unbinding Isaac. He looks upward. I can see tears streaming down his face.
FENDAL:	What's that noise? It sounds like a ram bleating. But where is it coming from?
SIGEN:	The bushes. I see it now. There's a ram caught by its horns. Abraham is going to it. Look!
FENDAL:	That's it! The sacrifice!
SIGEN:	I can't believe what I've just seen.
FENDAL:	Certainly no one can doubt Abraham's faith and obedience.
SIGEN:	Nor the promise that he and his descendants will find glory and favor . . . .
FENDAL:	Yes, but only if they keep the Covenant like Abraham. If they lose faith, or become disobedient, trials and suffering will mark their way.

Kush: Africa's Oldest Interior Empire

> ## Characters
>
> **MALAND**, a young Kushite boy
> **TARIK**, Maland's teenage brother
> **SANNA**, Maland's teenage sister
>
> **MANUTE, SORBA, JOMO**, Kushite soldiers
> **OPER**, a Kushite boy
> **YAPPA**, an elderly Kushite
> **TRUBU**, a Kushite teenage girl

Scene I: The Nile River, Kingdom of Kush, c. 1700 B.C.

MALAND:	What's *that* floating up the Nile?
TARIK:	Little brother . . . don't you know?
SANNA:	They come by here *all* the time.
MALAND:	Just because I'm younger than you, don't think I'm stupid. I know it's a barge. But whose?
TARIK:	It's an Egyptian, from far, far away.
MALAND:	How far?
SANNA:	Many days on the Nile.
MALAND:	Why would Egyptians travel so far? Are they visiting relatives?
TARIK:	Hardly. Just look at us. Our skins are much darker than theirs. I don't think they have relatives in Kush.
MALAND:	Then why do they come here?

SANNA:	Because we have things the Egyptians need and want.
MALAND:	Like what?
TARIK:	Ivory, gold, cattle, and timber and granite for their buildings.
MALAND:	Do our people give them these things?
TARIK:	It's very complicated, Maland. It's time for your nap now.
MALAND:	No! No! No! I want to know if the Egyptians steal from us.
SANNA:	Sometimes . . . when they are very strong. When they are weak and we are strong, they . . . trade more fairly.
MALAND:	They shouldn't steal from us! They should always trade fairly.
TARIK:	The Egyptians do whatever they think they can get away with. They feel we are part of *their* kingdom.
SANNA:	But we aren't! They've tried many times to conquer us, but have never succeeded.
TARIK:	But they keep trying. I've heard the Egyptians are planning to build more forts nearby.
MALAND:	They better watch out! Some day I'm going to Egypt with my friends and conquer all of them!
SANNA:	It sure is time for your nap now, little brother. You just go to sleep dreaming about Kush conquering mighty Egypt.

Scene II: Kushite boat, near Memphis, Egypt, c. 730 B.C.

MANUTE:	Well, men, what do you think our chances are?

SORBA:	What do you mean, chances? This will be like a contest with young children.
MANUTE:	What? Did you have your head under the boat? We're attacking Memphis! The capital! Can't you see those walls?
JOMO:	They're big, all right. But behind them wait only tired and demoralized soldiers.
MANUTE:	You both must have put your heads under water! Now one of you can see through walls!
SORBA:	Jomo knows what he's talking about. Our former leader Kashta crushed their fighting spirit when he conquered Upper Egypt.
JOMO:	Now Piankhy is ready to finish the Kush conquest of all Egypt.
MANUTE:	Wait a minute! This must be their last stronghold. Won't that cause them to fight more bravely?
SORBA:	Ha! When they see our fiery and determined eyes . . . set in our dark faces . . . they'll scatter like sheep before a lion!
MANUTE:	How can you say that? Egypt is a mighty country!
JOMO:	*Was* . . . you mean. They're a degenerate group now.
SORBA:	That's right. Their nobles and priests are forever feuding, destroying the last threads of Egyptian unity.
JOMO:	And don't forget . . . when they needed policemen, when they needed tough troops to kick out the Hyksos, whom did they call?
SORBA:	Us! Their dark-skinned neighbors!
JOMO:	They've looked down their noses at us for centuries . . .
SORBA:	. . . exploited our people and wealth . . .

JOMO:	Well, mighty Egypt, Kush is about to take you over!
	(A horn sounds.)
MANUTE:	There's the attack signal!

Scene III: Meröe, Kingdom of Kush, c. 500 B.C.

OPER:	Grandpa, may we ask you a question?
YAPPA:	Of course. If it's about something old, well, I'm an expert.
TRUBU:	It is. Where did our pyramids come from?
YAPPA:	Why, your ancestors built them.
OPER:	Coby says the Egyptians built them. That our people only did the muscle and sweat work.
YAPPA:	Coby should be ashamed of himself . . . two times, in fact.
TRUBU:	Two times?
YAPPA:	Yes. Once for underestimating his own people's skills and achievements . . .
OPER:	What do you mean by "underestimating"?
YAPPA:	Just look about our beautiful capital. Do you see a primitive and backward city? Of course not. We have magnificent public buildings—built by our people—an advanced iron smelting industry, and thriving markets with products from Arabia, India, and Africa.
OPER:	Yes . . . I understand what you mean.
TRUBU:	You said Coby should be ashamed two times. What's the other time?

YAPPA: For not knowing his history!

TRUBU: You mean, concerning the Egyptians?

YAPPA: Right. But first you must realize that when different peoples and cultures meet, they always end up borrowing from each other. Our ancestors took much from the Egyptians, especially ideas.

OPER: For instance . . .

YAPPA: Religious ideas, a written language, architecture . . .

TRUBU: What did the Egyptians take from us?

YAPPA: Many of our products, like gold, ivory, and granite. And our people, too, for soldiers and policemen. The Egyptians tried many times to conquer us, but failed. We Kushites finally conquered them!

OPER: Really? Tell us more.

YAPPA: Our armies overran theirs and our leaders became their pharaohs. At one time the Empire of Kush stretched from the Mediterranean Sea to Ethiopia.

TRUBU: How long did this great empire last?

YAPPA: Almost one hundred years.

OPER: Why didn't it last longer?

YAPPA: The great Assyrian armies from the East conquered Egypt, and our people returned to Kush.

TRUBU: How were the Assyrians able to do this? I thought Kushites were great fighters.

YAPPA: They were, but the Assyrians had superior weapons . . . made of iron!

OPER: But we have iron weapons and tools!

YAPPA: Today, yes, but not then. Anyway, though the Assyrians defeated our armies, our people won a kind of victory.

TRUBU: Grandpa, you don't make sense. How can you get a victory from a defeat and retreat?

YAPPA: We learned how to make iron from the Assyrians! Just as we learned how to build pyramids from the Egyptians.

OPER: I see. Are you now going to tell us what this teaches us?

YAPPA: How about one of you figuring it out?

TRUBU: Let me try . . . . A wise culture is always ready to learn new ideas and skills from others . . . that will strengthen and improve itself.

YAPPA: Excellent! You've just demonstrated your own profound conclusion!

Hammurabi and His Law Code

Characters

GOLIP, a royal aide
HAMMURABI,
  a Babylonian king
SARGIS, a Babylonian
  general

ZEEN, a royal adviser
TORL and MAMINT, farmers
JUDGE

Scene I: Royal Babylonian court,
c. 1760 B.C.

GOLIP: King Hammurabi, General Sargis has arrived.

HAMMURABI: Good. I trust he brings good news from the battlefield.

(Enter SARGIS.)

SARGIS: Victory is complete! The kingdom is again unified.

HAMMURABI: Excellent! I congratulate you, General Sargis, on this notable achievement. But I must add, this only means the empire is united in the military sense.

SARGIS: What do you mean, "only in the military sense"? All the empire's enemies are defeated!

HAMMURABI: Only the foreign ones. True unity, the kind that brings harmony and prosperity, is not found at the tip of a soldier's spear. It comes from within the people.

SARGIS: Do you mean a common religion for all?

GOLIP: That's one vital ingredient. The king will insist on a unity of religious beliefs.

SARGIS:	Where is this discussion going? I'm confused.
ZEEN:	Let's analyze unity from a general's perspective.
SARGIS:	I can certainly handle that. Go on.
ZEEN:	Besides simple fear, what causes all the people under your command, from foot soldier to general, to follow your orders?
SARGIS:	Respect.
ZEEN:	And for a soldier, what's the mother of respect?
SARGIS:	The conviction and feeling he's always being treated fairly . . . not abused or picked on without a just reason.
ZEEN:	What about punishment?
SARGIS:	He knows what it will be before the wrongdoing is committed.
HAMMURABI:	General, we'll make a legal scholar out of you yet!
SARGIS:	What are you talking about?
HAMMURABI:	Creating the right legal system. More than anything else, it will promote unity.
ZEEN:	At present, the empire has so many laws, customs, and regulations, that the people are confused.
GOLIP:	Some laws are written, many are not.
SARGIS:	So? What's the problem? Any king knows his first duty is to enforce the laws.
ZEEN:	Of course! Now, the real question is, what's the most efficient way of enforcing the law?
GOLIP:	Should we have troops pointing their spears in every street, shop, home, and farm?

SARGIS:	Of course not! You'd need too many guards. That's very expensive, and besides . . . who would watch all of them?
HAMMURABI:	Brilliant! Now we're getting somewhere. We need a system that causes the people themselves to enforce the laws . . . an inner authority pointing the way.
SARGIS:	And not external spear tips. But how do you create that inner authority in people?
HAMMURABI:	By creating a simple, yet comprehensive code of laws that all the people can learn and understand. No more guessing.
ZEEN:	King Hammurabi has formed a special commission to do exactly that. They've already started.
GOLIP:	The code will deal with issues of property, business and trade, labor, the family, injuries, and of course, criminal acts like murder and theft. And the military as well . . .
ZEEN:	Most of these laws and regulations are centuries old. There's much continuity with the past.
HAMMURABI:	And that gives the people a sense of security and confidence.
SARGIS:	But will knowledge of the laws alone create that "inner authority"?
HAMMURABI:	Another excellent insight, General Sargis. Like your troops, the people must believe in the code, and not just fear it.
ZEEN:	The king is most insistent that the code be seen by all as something just and fair.
GOLIP:	That the weak are secure in the knowledge that the code protects them from oppression by the strong.
ZEEN:	That even if robbers take all their possessions, and are not caught, the government will make full compensation to the victims.

24 Exciting Plays for Ancient History Classes

SARGIS:	Now I'm beginning to understand how this inner authority is created. People will respect and obey laws that they believe are fair and just, and that protect their interests.
GOLIP:	That's the ideal, but we're far, far from it.
HAMMURABI:	Of course, we realize that only fear of punishment makes *some* people obey the law.
ZEEN:	The code is based on equivalent retaliation.
SARGIS:	Give me an example.
GOLIP:	Let's say you hire someone to build your house. Upon completion, you move in, and then one day the roof collapses and kills you. Punishment to the builder is equivalent retaliation: death.
ZEEN:	If a patient dies from a surgery, the doctor responsible has his fingers cut off.
SARGIS:	What are some other crimes punishable by death?
GOLIP:	Rape, kidnapping, burglary, and corruption by a government official, to name a few.
SARGIS:	Some of these punishments seem very severe. Aren't you concerned that people will lose respect for the code because of this harshness?
HAMMURABI:	Let's go back to the reason for the code. We want to create a unified, orderly, stable, and just society, one in which the people's welfare will improve.
ZEEN:	Knowing the dire consequences of negligent actions, people like surgeons and builders will be very careful in their work.
HAMMURABI:	The code will foster fairness in trade and competence in the professions. All this will cause the people to feel confident in their personal and business affairs.

24 Exciting Plays for Ancient History Classes

GOLIP:	The code tries to eliminate all the shady and dark places where the strong and smart can take advantage of the weak and simple.
SARGIS:	Wait a bit! I see a real danger here. What if I accuse my neighbor falsely? What if I make up something just because I can't stand him? What's to protect my neighbor?
HAMMURABI:	The very first law of the code: If someone brings charges he can't prove, he himself is punished of the charge.
SARGIS:	That will certainly discourage people from chasing off to court too quickly.
HAMMURABI:	Precisely. The code is intended to discourage lawsuits. People should work things out themselves, and only come to court as a last resort.
SARGIS:	Who will run the courts? Priests?
HAMMURABI:	Definitely not. We want the law enforced as it reads.
SARGIS:	If the priests are excluded, won't they make serious trouble?
HAMMURABI:	The people will be told that this code was given by the god Marduk, and therefore, it does not need priestly interpretation.
SARGIS:	Divinely sanctioned laws . . . with the priests out of the picture . . . very wise.

Scene II: Rural Babylonia, a few years later.

TORL:	Rainy season's almost here. Do you think we'll get a lot, like last year?
MAMINT:	If we do, I hope that dike of yours holds.
TORL:	What are you talking about?

24 Exciting Plays for Ancient History Classes

MAMINT:	I'll show you . . . look for yourself. It seems to me it needs some serious attention.
TORL:	Well, neighbor, it seems to me you should mind your own business. And you can begin by keeping your fuzzy-faced son away from my daughter!
MAMINT:	Hold on! Your rotten dike *is* my business. If it breaks, all my land will be flooded and I'll lose my crop.
TORL:	And your little woman will chase you back to your mother's.
MAMINT:	You've been drinking too much beer again.
TORL:	I said, mind your own business, neighbor!
MAMINT:	Don't say I didn't warn you.

Scene III: Royal Babylonian court, a few months later.

JUDGE:	Next case: Mamint versus Torl. Mamint, as the plaintiff, do you understand your responsibilities?
MAMINT:	I do.
JUDGE:	What is the nature of your charge?
MAMINT:	My neighbor Torl, did not properly maintain his dike. When it broke, my crop was ruined.
JUDGE:	Torl, what is your response to the accusation?
TORL:	He doesn't know what he's talking about! The dike was in good condition. It just had an unnatural amount of stress on it because of all the rain this year.
JUDGE:	We certainly did get a lot of rain. And that makes this a most difficult case. I assume the dike was completely broken.

24 Exciting Plays for Ancient History Classes

MAMINT:	That's right, judge.
JUDGE:	A broken dike does not necessarily mean negligence, nor can it be easily examined, like a collapsed roof. Mamint, I can only rule in your favor if you can prove the dike needed repairs before the rains came.
TORL:	He can't! It's my good word against his . . . the whining, half-blind wimp!
JUDGE:	I'll advise you to discuss only facts and not feelings, Torl. Now, Mamint, do you have any response? Any proof or testimony?
MAMINT:	I foresaw this problem and I confronted Torl with the dike's condition. This was weeks before the rainy season began. Since I didn't think he would fix it on time, I asked a government engineer to inspect the dike. Here's his report, with an official seal of place and *time*.
JUDGE:	The dike was examined before the rainy season, and needed serious repairs . . . . Very well, by the great Law of Hammurabi, you, Torl, are to compensate Mamint, for the full and legal amount of his lost crop. Government officials will assess the proper amount. And you are to return the broken dike to proper working condition within three months.
TORL:	But I don't have that kind of money!
JUDGE:	Then you shall forfeit your farm and all possessions to your neighbor Mamint.
TORL:	Never! I'll come up with the payment.
JUDGE:	Very well. You also have three months to pay this off in full, half within thirty days. And don't forget the dike's repair. Next case . . . .
MAMINT:	Well, neighbor, it looks like Hammurabi's Code does work for a poor farmer like myself.
TORL:	If your lout of a son bothers my beautiful daughter again, I'll put that code to use myself! And don't worry . . . you'll get your money. Just don't send your boy over for it!

The Shang Dynasty: The Birth of Chinese Civilization

Scene I: Shang territory, ancient China, c. 1600 B.C.

KAO: Greetings, great Lord of Shang.

TANG: Welcome, visitors. How may I serve you?

CHUN: Do you know about King Jie?

TANG: He is of your Xia dynasty.

KAO: We are very concerned about him. He is certain to forfeit the Mandate of Heaven. If something is not done, our people will suffer greatly.

TANG: What has King Jie done?

CHUN: He has become an absolute tyrant.

KAO: His personal behavior dishonors our sacred ancestors.

CHUN: He and his consort engage in unspeakable amusements.

TANG: In private quarters?

KAO: No, no. He made his servants build a lake filled with wine. He forces hundreds of his subjects to dive into the wine until they all become sickly drunk.

TANG: If the king has become so corrupt and abusive, why journey so far to see me? Someone in the royal court should deal with this matter.

CHUN: They, too, are corrupt.

KAO: Or afraid to act.

CHUN: We know you are a strong and honorable leader . . .

KAO: Who will not humiliate his subjects or disgrace our sacred ancestors . . .

CHUN: Whose behavior merits the Mandate of Heaven . . . .

TANG: Are you asking me to challenge the king? To begin a new dynasty?

CHUN: We are! A civilized and honorable one!

TANG: But many will defend the old king. Do you have war chariots and bronze weapons?

KAO: What are they?

TANG: I'm glad you don't know. I will not ask the Shang people to fight without a heavenly sign.

CHUN: You have our complete support. The oracles will tell you this is right. Then you will fight with your war chariots and bronze to victory!

KAO: And boldly claim the Mandate of Heaven!

CHUN: And begin your just rule . . . as first king of the Shang Dynasty!

Scene II: Aristocrat's home, Anyang, c. 1200 B.C.

WO: I am an official of King Wu Ding's Royal Court. I wish to speak with Zeng about his son, Li.

JIANG: I am Li's mother. Tell me your business.

WO: I . . . I . . . will not speak to a woman regarding this official matter.

(Enter ZENG.)

ZENG: I have overheard this conversation. Show the proper respect for Li's mother, and speak to her about our son.

WO: But . . . but . . .

ZENG: But nothing! Are you from so far away that you do not know of the high status that women of the nobility have in Shang society? State your business, please.

WO: Very well. Please forgive me. I was born far from here, and I am new to this position.

JIANG: We forgive you.

WO: Your son has shown himself to be quick of mind, keen of speech, and very skilled with his hands. The Royal Court wants Li to immediately begin training in our written language.

ZENG: There are over a thousand different characters!

WO: The teachers are confident he can master this challenge.

JIANG: Does this mean Li will one day become a diviner of the oracle bones?

WO: What do you mean?

ZENG: You *are* new.

JIANG: If the king wants to know the answer to an important
                 question, such as where and when he should hunt, the
                 question is written on a special animal bone. Later, great
                 heat is applied, causing cracks.

ZENG: The diviner then reads these cracks as answers from our
                 ancestors' spirits.

WO: Of course . . . . I just didn't hear you clearly.

JIANG: Our son will not be a diviner.

WO: No, now I remember . . . . Li is to begin training in writing
                 history.

ZENG: We are pleased. I will get my son.

Scene III: Royal writing school, Anyang, years later.

LI: I have finished recording the king's hunt.

HUI: Let me see . . . . Excellent, excellent work.

LI: You are a patient and gifted teacher.

HUI: And you, Li, are a most remarkable student. You have
                 mastered all the basic pictograms and complex ideograms.
                 And no student is more skilled in writing the difficult homo-
                 phones than you.

LI: Writing our language gives me great pleasure.

HUI: Yes, I can see that. Now, I have a new challenge for you.
                 Instead of writing on bones, bamboo, or silk, you will learn to
                 make inscriptions on bronze.

LI: Bronze? Here? Who will be my teacher?

HUI:	Slow down. You will study at the royal foundry. Soong, the master caster and foundry overseer, will be your teacher and guide.
LI:	When do I begin?
HUI:	Tomorrow. They have an important project starting, and need your hand right away.
LI:	Thank you for all you've taught me. I will work hard and well to make you proud.
HUI:	I know you will. I will escort you myself to the foundry. We'll leave at dawn.

Scene IV: Royal bronze foundry, Anyang, next day.

SOONG:	Welcome Hui, my old friend. This must be Li, your prize student.
HUI:	Yes. It's good to see you again, my friend. May we have a tour of the foundry?
SOONG:	Of course. Li, do you realize how important bronze making has been to the Shang Dynasty?
LI:	I think so.
SOONG:	By having a royal monopoly, the kings have become powerful and wealthy.
LI:	I see. What do you make here?
SOONG:	Everything from small goblets and pitchers to giant cauldrons.
LI:	How large is a "giant" cauldron?
SOONG:	Come with me and I'll show you . . . . These workers are about to cast one that will weigh nearly a ton.

24 Exciting Plays for Ancient History Classes

LI: A ton! How could they possibly do that?

SOONG: Over the years we've become very sophisticated in metallurgy. Experience has enabled us to coordinate the efforts of several hundred skilled workers.

HUI: It looks like quite a few are involved in this particular casting.

SOONG: That's right. This is an especially tricky cast, besides being a very heavy one. A wrong move at any step in the process and we could have a complete disaster.

LI: What's this cauldron going to be used for?

SOONG: Special religious ceremonies at the palace.

HUI: What's the project Li will be working on?

SOONG: Inscribing a dragon-figure vessel.

LI: For the king?

SOONG: In a way. Fu Hou, the king's consort, has died, and many valuable articles will be buried with her.

LI: For instance . . .

SOONG: Many bronze vessels, bells, chimes, and drums, possibly even a chariot as well.

LI: When do I start?

SOONG: After you've mastered mold-making. We'll get started on that right away.

LI: I'm ready. I just hope I can take the heat.

SOONG: Of the furnaces, or of the job's high expectations?

LI: Both, I guess.

HUI: Let me relieve your anxiety. You'll find my friend Soong to be an expert craftsman, and a patient and understanding teacher.

LI: As you have been.

HUI: All he expects is your full cooperation and obedience.

LI: Of course. Isn't that our way?

Crete, Home of Europe's First Civilization: The Minoan

Characters

RENALUS, a Minoan merchant
ARIAD, his wife

LATIK, a copper merchant
SEJJ, a tin merchant

Scene I: Merchant's home, Phaistos, Crete, c. 1455 B.C.

RENALUS: Dear, I'm bringing home two very important clients next week. They'll be staying with us for a few days.

ARIAD: What? How could you? The house is a disaster with all the painters coming and going.

RENALUS: By the way . . . how are the new frescoes coming along?

ARIAD: You must be kidding. Have you forgotten, or is your mind only capable of thinking in terms of exports and imports?

RENALUS: Dearest wife, what are you talking about?

ARIAD: Before you left for your last business trip we still couldn't agree on the frescoes.

RENALUS: Yes, now I remember. I wanted pictures of bull-leaping and boxing. You wanted dolphins swimming in the bright blue sea. What's the verdict?

ARIAD: We don't have one!

RENALUS: Then, let's compromise . . . and you take care of the details.

ARIAD:	Fine. Now, about your guests coming . . .
RENALUS:	I know it's a great bother and inconvenience, but this is very, I mean, *very* important.
ARIAD:	I think I've heard that one before.
RENALUS:	Dear, you know how crucial bronze is to our Minoan economy . . . and that we have no copper or tin in Crete.
ARIAD:	And these two are very, I mean, *very* big suppliers.
RENALUS:	That's right!
ARIAD:	So cultivating their goodwill with hospitality is smart—and necessary business.
RENALUS:	Spoken like a true Minoan merchant's wife.
ARIAD:	Will they be staying only here while in Crete?
RENALUS:	No. They want to see our capital.
ARIAD:	And so do I! I'll have the house ready for them. But just remember . . . you're not going to Knossos without me. I have some serious shopping and sightseeing to do there myself.
RENALUS:	Anything else, dear?
ARIAD:	Have you checked all the pithoi lately? We'll need plenty of food, drink, and oil for our guests.
RENALUS:	We can't be low already. I just had those jars filled, and they're all taller than I am.
ARIAD:	Very well. If we run out when your very important clients are here, don't blame me or the servants.

Scene II: Days later.

RENALUS:	Dear, our guests have arrived. This is Latik from Cyprus, and Sejj from Asia Minor.

ARIAD:	It's an honor to open our home to such important visitors.
LATIK:	The honor is all ours. Here is a gift in appreciation of your generous hospitality . . .
SEJJ:	And a tribute to your great beauty.
ARIAD:	You are both so kind and thoughtful. Thank you.
LATIK:	It is a rare and great pleasure for us to socialize with a woman.
SEJJ:	Where we come from, the sexes are always separated.
RENALUS:	Not in Crete. You'll see women everywhere.
LATIK:	So we have observed. Tell us, why do your women have such fair skin and wear beautiful clothes, while your men look like the copper I sell, and dress rather plainly?
RENALUS:	I suppose because we're always hard at work.
ARIAD:	Watch it, dear husband.
SEJJ:	I'm sorry . . . we did not intend to stir up a hornet's nest.
ARIAD:	Nothing of the kind. We debate all the time and keep on good terms. Now, let me show you two the house and where you'll stay.
LATIK:	House? This is a palace! It's beautiful!
ARIAD:	Compared to the great homes of Knossos, this is rather modest.
SEJJ:	Ha! Our homes on the mainland are primitive huts compared to this.
LATIK:	How did your builders achieve such engineering feats . . .

24 Exciting Plays for Ancient History Classes

SEJJ: As this staircase and three stories?

ARIAD: They've had lots of practice.

LATIK: What do you mean by that?

RENALUS: My wife is referring to our frequent earthquakes. A few hundred years ago earthquakes destroyed all our great palaces.

ARIAD: Instead of moving elsewhere, we Minoans simply built them more grand.

SEJJ: Your interior walls are so bright and beautiful! This painting of dolphins is so colorful, so fresh and natural looking.

LATIK: By comparison, our art seems dull and stiff.

ARIAD: Why, thank you. These are special paintings called "frescoes."

RENALUS: Hmm. Dear . . . where are my pictures of boxers and bull-leapers?

ARIAD: Oh . . . Follow me, please, to the men's bathroom.

RENALUS: I just knew she'd have them painted there!

SEJJ: What's this? I've never seen anything like it!

RENALUS: Here's where the water comes in . . . and there are the pipes that drain it away. We're very proud of our plumbing system.

LATIK: Do you mean you can bring fresh water into this room, and drain it away after using it? In my home we have to haul it to and fro in earthen jars. It's a back-breaking job.

ARIAD: See for yourself. We Minoans love beautiful things, but above all, we love what is practical and efficient.

RENALUS:	Some people say our ships and plumbing best represent our culture.
ARIAD:	I'd say it's our art and architecture.
SEJJ:	What about your leisure and entertainment activities?
RENALUS:	They tell a lot about us, too. When we're in the capital, you'll see bull-leaping at its best. It's our favorite amusement. I've already reserved our seats.
ARIAD:	I hope you can still count to four. Don't forget who's coming along . . . .

Scene III: Royal palace, Knossos, Crete, days later.

LATIK:	Your capital is immense! How many inhabitants?
RENALUS:	At least 80,000.
SEJJ:	Amazing! It must be the greatest city in the world!
RENALUS:	I'll leave that judgment to others . . . but I believe you'll find our entertainment as graceful and pulse-stopping as our great city.
LATIK:	You mean the bull-leaping? What exactly is it?
RENALUS:	Once we're in our seats we'll explain. Follow me.
	(They enter the stadium.)
ARIAD:	What do you see in the ring?
LATIK:	Three very trim and athletic-looking youths. Two females and one male, each about 16 years old.

SEJJ:	Now they're all doing flips and somersaults. I can't believe how agile they are!
RENALUS:	They're just warming up. Now, all is ready!
ARIAD:	When the bull is loose, one of the team will dive between its horns, do a half flip onto the bull's back, push off with her hands, and make another half flip into the waiting arms of the catcher.
RENALUS:	All in about one second.
LATIK:	No! Impossible! Unless the bull remains still it can't be done!
RENALUS:	Just watch!
SEJJ:	That bull won't stay still. Look at him charge!
LATIK:	I can't look.
SEJJ:	She did it! Right through the horns of the charging bull!
ARIAD:	The three will now switch roles—leaper, catcher, and next leaper—and do it again.
LATIK:	Amazing! Do they ever get hurt?
ARIAD:	Yes, when they are not careful.
SEJJ:	Speaking of being careful, don't you Minoans worry about the growing power of the mainland Mycenaeans?
RENALUS:	I don't follow you.
SEJJ:	You have such a prosperous and advanced culture . . . a most inviting treasure to foreigners.
LATIK:	But we've seen no walls protecting your cities. The great fort at Mycenae looks like giants built it!

SEJJ: Yes. It's the one with the Lions Gate.

ARIAD: The great cliffs of our island serve as fortress walls. We are not anxious.

LATIK: But the Mycenaeans are very aggressive, very warlike. You Minoans live for beauty and refinement. Mycenaeans live for conquest!

RENALUS: Have you forgotten about our great fleet? It is most formidable and experienced.

ARIAD: It's kept out invaders for many, many years.

RENALUS: And cleaned the Aegean of pirates who used to threaten our merchant ships.

ARIAD: Besides, why should the Mycenaeans want to invade us? We've traded peacefully with them for a long time.

RENALUS: In fact, many of them live here. We interact with them all the time.

SEJJ: All the same, I don't trust them. They remind me of the bull we just saw. They'll take advantage of any weakness . . . so be on your guard!

RENALUS: Enough serious talk. Let's eat!

24 Exciting Plays for Ancient History Classes

The Israelites Flee Egypt and Receive the Law

Characters

NAIN and ABIDA,
Hebrew men
ZILPAH and MILCAH,
Hebrew women
MOSES

AARON
PHARAOH
JETHRO

Scene I: Egyptian construction site, c. 1400–1200 B.C.

NAIN: Abida, I can't take this kind of life any longer.

ABIDA: What do you mean? We have food, shelter, and jobs.

NAIN: And stripes on our backs from the overseer's quick lash. Face the facts: we can never improve our lives here. Our Egyptian masters are never satisfied. We'll always be their slaves.

ABIDA: Such is our fate, so accept it. Take pride in the great buildings we have made.

NAIN: They are not ours, and I will not accept my fate. I have heard the stories our old men tell about our people . . . .

ABIDA: Yes . . . I know them, too . . . how our people long ago left the land promised to Abraham.

NAIN: The land flowing with milk and honey.

ABIDA: But not in the days of Jacob. Famine gripped the land and his sons came here to Egypt.

NAIN:	Why did they stay? Famines don't last forever.
ABIDA:	I don't know. Maybe our ancestors became enchanted by the Egyptians' way of life: their majestic buildings, luxurious clothes and jewelry, great achievements in science and agriculture . . . .
NAIN:	What? Our people live no better than stray dogs! When did we ever enjoy the fruits of Egyptian civilization?
ABIDA:	Many, many years ago, when Jacob's son, Joseph, held a high position in Pharaoh's court. But as our people grew in number the pharaohs feared we'd one day take over. So they took our rights and privileges away.
NAIN:	How could the Egyptians do that?
ABIDA:	Simple. There were no laws to protect us.
NAIN:	Look busy. Here comes the overseer with his whip.

Scene II: A small dark hut in the Hebrew settlement.

ZILPAH:	Milcah, why do you look so troubled?
MILCAH:	Oh, Zilpah . . . there is talk that the Egyptians are going to take our sons. What will they do to them?
ZILPAH:	Do not believe every rumor . . . but many years ago they tried to kill every male Hebrew baby.

Scene III: The Pharaoh's court.

PHARAOH:	Aides! Who are these presumptuous old men you have brought before me?
AARON:	I am Aaron, and this is my brother.

MOSES:	The Lord God of Israel commands you to free His people!
PHARAOH:	What are you babbling about? Do you know whom you are addressing, old man?
AARON:	Obey, or Egypt will suffer greatly.
PHARAOH:	You two and your tribal god cannot threaten me! Guards, take them away at once! I'll show those complaining Hebrews who has power to command!

Scene IV: Hebrew settlement, late in the day, days later.

ZILPAH:	What is happening? Are we all doomed? Plague after plague . . . . Water turned to blood . . . frogs, gnats, flies, and locusts without number. Skin boils and hail . . . . Why?
MILCAH:	To move the Pharaoh's heart to release us from bondage. Remember, only the Egyptians have suffered.
ZILPAH:	But this is our home.
	(Enter NAIN and ABIDA.)
NAIN:	No it is not!
ABIDA:	The nine plagues have not moved the Pharaoh.
NAIN:	One more comes: death.
ABIDA:	We have been instructed to place lamb's blood on the sides and tops of our doorways—
NAIN:	To guide the Angel of Death to pass over and spare our people.
ABIDA:	When Egyptian sons die, the Pharaoh will let us go.
NAIN:	But we must leave quickly. He might change his mind.

Scene V: Near Mt. Horeb, many days later.

MOSES: Aaron, my brother, I am weary. The people do nothing but complain.

AARON: They are impatient for the Promised Land.

MOSES: Who approaches our camp?

JETHRO: It is Jethro, your father-in-law. Moses, I have heard of your great accomplishments.

MOSES: Would that the people remember and appreciate them. Everyone wants my attention. I cannot solve every problem. The people are growing more and more restless. Worry and fatigue are overcoming me.

JETHRO: Moses, my son. Reduce your burden. Find honest and righteous men to handle problems as they arise. Concern yourself only with the biggest and lasting ones. Organize and delegate your authority.

MOSES: Jethro, thank you for this wise counsel. But such men and I need something to guide our judgments . . . a fair and just code the people will respect and accept. Something from our God.

Scene VI: Israelites' camp near Mt. Sinai.

ZILPAH: Why do we remain camped here?

MILCAH: Moses and Aaron have climbed Mt. Sinai for a revelation.

ZILPAH: A revelation? Of what?

MILCAH: I'm not certain. But the talk in the camp says it's very important. It will determine who we are as a people.

(Enter NAIN and ABIDA.)

NAIN:	Moses and Aaron have returned.
ABIDA:	They have brought from the Most High, the Law.
NAIN:	Ten basic commandments.
MILCAH:	What do they say?
NAIN:	Four of them concern our relationship with our God.
ABIDA:	The other six tell us how we are to treat each other as people.
NAIN:	As people . . . all who are equal before the Law.
ABIDA:	The Ten Commandments are truly from the Most High. They are so clear, direct, and beautiful.
NAIN:	If we follow and obey them, we will be a blessed people.
ZILPAH:	The Egyptians have their pyramids. I hope and pray these commandments shall be our treasure forevermore.

Ruth of the Old Testament

Characters

ORPAH, a Moabite widow
NAOMI, a Hebrew widow
RUTH, a Moabite widow

FOREMAN (for Boaz)
BOAZ, a Hebrew kinsman-
redeemer

Scene I: Moab, c. 1150 B.C.

ORPAH: Mother, why are you gathering all your possessions?

NAOMI: I'm returning to the land of my people.

RUTH: But Judah is a place of famine and suffering.

NAOMI: Not anymore. I've heard food and plenty have returned there. Besides, Moab is only a place of death, sorrow, and bitterness for me now. My husband and two sons are buried here.

ORPAH: We share your grief, for your sons were our dear husbands. Stay with us, and we will look after all your needs.

NAOMI: No. I am going home. You two are still young. Find a new life here amongst your own people.

RUTH: The journey to Bethlehem is long and difficult.

ORPAH: We will not let you undertake it alone.

NAOMI: You have been wonderful daughters-in-law. But that time has passed. Go find new husbands.

ORPAH: We are going with you.

(They walk some distance.)

NAOMI: I'll have no more of this. There's no life for you where I'm going. You'll only become despised and exploited aliens. Return to your families.

(ORPAH kisses NAOMI farewell and returns.)

ORPAH: Good-bye, dear Mother.

NAOMI: Ruth, Ruth, why do you cling to me so? You have already shown enough love and devotion. Now, follow after Orpah.

RUTH: No. I'm going with you all the way.

NAOMI: But you don't know what that means.

RUTH: No, I don't, but wherever you go, I will follow.

NAOMI: But I am a Hebrew, and you are a Gentile . . . .

RUTH: Your people will be my people.

NAOMI: We worship the one true God. Your people—

RUTH: Your God will be my God.

NAOMI: I am old. When I die, surely you will return home to your people.

RUTH: My home is with you, and your people, and your God. Where you are buried, there also will be my final resting place.

NAOMI: Life will be very difficult for us.

RUTH: I have faith in the God of Abraham and Isaac.

Scene II: NAOMI's house in Bethlehem, some days later.

NAOMI: There is no more food. We will starve, unless . . . .

RUTH: I will go out and glean. We have the right, do we not?

NAOMI: Yes. Moses commanded the wealthy farmers to leave some grain behind for the poor to glean. Be careful!

Scene III: Fields of BOAZ, a short time later.

FOREMAN: Welcome, Master. The Lord bless you!

BOAZ: And the Lord bless you as well. How is the harvest coming along?

FOREMAN: Very well. It's going to be a prosperous year.

BOAZ: How many gleaners?

FOREMAN: About the usual numbers.

BOAZ: Who is that young woman over there? I don't recognize her.

FOREMAN: A newcomer, a very pleasant and appreciative Moabite woman. She's been hard at work since sunup.

BOAZ: What connection would she have with Bethlehem?

FOREMAN: She's the widowed daughter-in-law of Naomi. They both recently came from Moab.

BOAZ: Oh, so she's the one. I've heard about her great devotion to Naomi. Make sure she has plenty to glean . . . and that no man touches her.

FOREMAN:	Whatever you command, Master. Though she is a Gentile, I sense she's a woman of great virtue and integrity.
BOAZ:	Yes, and I mean to be her protector. *(BOAZ goes to RUTH in the fields.)*
RUTH:	If you are the owner of these fields, I am most grateful to you.
BOAZ:	I am. I am Boaz. Do not glean in any other man's fields. I will provide for you, and protect you here from any lustful hands.
RUTH:	Thank you . . . but why do you treat a foreigner like me with such kindness and generosity?
BOAZ:	I have heard of your unselfish love and devotion to your mother-in-law, Naomi. Now I should ask you the same question.
RUTH:	Should we only show kindness to a few people? Only to our friends and kin of like blood? Are we not all children of the same one and only God?
BOAZ:	Your thoughts are my thoughts. Come and share my meal.
RUTH:	I do not understand why you still treat me so kindly. You could easily exploit me—I am a poor, defenseless widow, and a foreigner. Other men of your wealth and position would take advantage.
BOAZ:	They are men without honor, who disgrace both themselves and their people. Their greed and lust bring only suffering and bitterness, discord and death. We were made for something better, something more noble than satisfying animal appetites.

Scene IV: NAOMI's home, hours later.

NAOMI:	Daughter, where did you get all this grain?

RUTH: In the fields of a kind and generous man—Boaz.

NAOMI: Boaz! The Lord is indeed kind and merciful! No more is my cup of hope empty! Ruth, Ruth, Boaz is one of our kinsman-redeemers!

RUTH: What do you mean?

NAOMI: My husband was related to him. A kinsman-redeemer is responsible for protecting all needy members of his extended family. What did he ask of you?

RUTH: To stay with his women workers until the harvest is complete.

NAOMI: Of course . . . . A beauty like you in another man's fields would be abused.

Scene V: NAOMI's home, days later.

RUTH: Mother, what are you doing with that perfume?

NAOMI: It is my turn to look after you. Tonight, Boaz will be at his threshing floor. Wash and perfume yourself, and put on your best clothes. Watch where he goes to sleep. Then go to him, uncover his feet, and lie down.

RUTH: I . . . I . . . don't understand.

NAOMI: Trust me. I know your heart and his. When Boaz awakes, he will tell you what to do. Now, go prepare yourself like a new bride.

Scene VI: BOAZ's threshing floor, that night.

BOAZ: What's that noise? . . . Who are you?

RUTH: Ruth, your servant. Spread the corner of your garment over me, since you are a kinsman-redeemer.

BOAZ:	Surely this is all a dream. What you have just asked brings me joy beyond words.
RUTH:	You and I are very much awake.
BOAZ:	But you could have chosen a much younger man to be your husband.
RUTH:	It was God's plan, and my heart's desire.
BOAZ:	But I cannot marry you until our customs have been fulfilled.
RUTH:	What do you mean?
BOAZ:	There's one closer in kinship to you than I. He has the first right to be your kinsman-redeemer.
RUTH:	What will you do?
BOAZ:	What is right. Go before the elders and publicly discuss the matter with this kinsman.
RUTH:	I pray he gives you this right.
BOAZ:	I will go to him first thing in the morning. But stay at my feet until then. To protect your honor, you should leave before anyone can see you.

EPILOGUE

Ruth and Boaz married, and had a son, Obed. Obed was the father of Jesse. Jesse was the father of David, Israel's greatest king.

The Life and Times of David

Characters

DAVID
KEIL and ATAB, Saul's
  servants
SAUL, first Hebrew king
JESSE, David's father
RUL, a Hebrew soldier

ELIAB, David's brother
GOLIATH, a Philistine
  champion
LETE and BOK, David's aides
NATHAN, a Hebrew prophet

Scene I: Hill country, near Bethlehem, c. 1025 B.C.

DAVID: *(singing)* "The Lord is my Shepherd, I—" Who goes there?

KEIL: Servants of King Saul.

ATAB: You play the harp and sing very well. Are you David, son of Jesse?

DAVID: I am.

KEIL: Our king is very upset. His mind and spirit are increasingly tormented.

ATAB: I have heard of your great musical talents. We would like you to play for the king in hopes of calming his angry nerves.

DAVID: I will if my father consents.

KEIL: We have just met with him, and he has agreed.

ATAB: Say, shepherd boy, does your harp calm the wild beasts so they don't attack your flocks? Ha!

KEIL: Atab, you insensitive slob!

ATAB: Hey, I was only joking.

DAVID: I have other ways of protecting the flocks.

Scene II: King SAUL's court, a few weeks later.

SAUL: David, keep playing . . . how your music soothes my restless spirit.

DAVID: My King, why are you so troubled?

SAUL: The prophet Samuel says I have angered the Lord. What does that old man know, anyway? I'm the king. Do you think my enemies, the Philistines, rest while I wait for Samuel to make the proper sacrifices? Ha! Sing to me.

DAVID: *(singing)* "Lift up your heads, O ye gates . . . and the King of glory shall come in. Who is this King of glory . . . ."

SAUL: *I'm* the king!

DAVID: *(singing)* "The Lord of Hosts, He is the King of glory."

Scene III: JESSE's home, Bethlehem, weeks later.

JESSE: David, my youngest son, go to your three oldest brothers with this food.

DAVID: Yes, Father.

JESSE: And bring back news from the battlefront. I pray the men of Israel will triumph.

© 1992 J. Weston Walch, Publisher

Scene IV: Valley of Elah (battlefront), a short time later.

DAVID: I'm looking for Eliab, Abinadab, and Shammah.

RUL: Over there.

ELIAB: David! What are you doing here? Who's minding the flocks? Go home. The battle could begin any time.

DAVID: Brother, why are you angry with me?

ELIAB: We're not battling the Philistines to give thrills to spectators! Now, go home!

RUL: Uh-oh . . . here he comes again.

DAVID: Who?

RUL: Goliath, the giant. He's the champion warrior of the Philistines. Every morning and evening he struts out to taunt and challenge us.

DAVID: What's his challenge?

RUL: Single combat with our champion. The loser's people become subjects to the winner's people. He's been doing this for forty continuous days.

DAVID: And none of our men have come forth?

RUL: Of course not! Look at Goliath. Do any of our men stand a chance against one so large and strong? We flee from his shadow.

DAVID: I wouldn't.

ELIAB: David! Don't mock us with your foolish bravado. Go home where you belong.

Scene V: King SAUL's camp, a short time later.

SAUL: David, my comfort, why are you here?

DAVID: To ask your permission to fight Goliath.

SAUL: Out of the question! You're a musician, and he's a seasoned killer.

DAVID: I have killed bears and lions that threatened my flocks!

SAUL: I sense you are very determined. Very well. I'll outfit you with the best armor and sword.

                     (DAVID tries on the armor, then sheds it.)

DAVID: This is too cumbersome. I can't fight a bear wearing a lion's hide.

                     (Walks to a stream where he gathers five pebbles.)

Scene VI: Battlefront with the Philistines.

GOLIATH: I'm here again, you Hebrew vermin! Where is your champion? Hey, you, boy! Get away!

DAVID: In the name of the Lord Almighty, whom you mock with the insults of an idiot, I take up your challenge.

GOLIATH: You? Do you think Goliath is a dog? You circumcised puppy! I'll crush your sweet face like fresh bread and feed it to the birds!

DAVID: The Lord will show He saves not by spear or sword—

GOLIATH: Oh, yeah, let's just see Him save you from this!

24 Exciting Plays for Ancient History Classes

(GOLIATH attacks. DAVID places one stone in his sling, fires, and fells GOLIATH with a shot to the forehead. DAVID runs to GOLIATH, decapitates him with his own sword, and then raises up GOLIATH's head.)

DAVID: You Philistines . . . regard now your champion!

(Israelite armies pursue the Philistines.)

Scene VII: DAVID's camp, Ziklag, 1010 B.C.

LETE: Where's David?

BOK: Alone, in deep mourning. He weeps and tears his clothes.

LETE: Why? For whom?

BOK: A messenger just informed him of King Saul's death. And his friend Jonathan is dead, too.

LETE: I can understand his tears for Jonathan. He was a true and loyal friend. But for Saul? How many times did he try to kill David? All because of jealousy.

BOK: David would never usurp the Lord's anointed.

LETE: What are his plans now that he is king?

BOK: Unite all the tribes of Israel under his kingship. Then drive out the Philistines and secure Jerusalem for the glory of the Lord.

LETE: Jerusalem? As David's capital?

BOK: Yes. He intends to make it the most beautiful city in the world, and to bring the Ark of the Covenant there to rest in a new and great temple.

LETE: What a dreamer. He'll never bring it off.

BOK:	David never confines his dreams to his couch. They move him, and he shakes us. No man is more confident in the Lord's power. Remember Goliath?

Scene VIII: DAVID's palace, Jerusalem, c. 995 B.C.

DAVID:	Nathan, good prophet, you wish to see me?
NATHAN:	The Lord has promised his servant, David, an everlasting dynasty.
DAVID:	He is my rock and refuge. I abide in Him. Your reasons for coming?
NATHAN:	To tell a story . . . . Once there was a very wealthy man with many goats and sheep. His neighbor, a poor man, owned but one little lamb. He loved that little lamb and raised it like a daughter amongst his own children.
DAVID:	I know the feeling, for I was a shepherd, too. Continue.
NATHAN:	A traveler came to the rich man, who decided to honor his guest with a feast. Instead of taking one of his own animals, the rich man took his poor neighbor's only lamb.
DAVID:	What? Surely there was a mistake. How could the rich man be so selfish and cruel?
NATHAN:	The poor man's pet was slaughtered, and—
DAVID:	Tell me no more! What a terrible injustice! The rich man deserves death!
NATHAN:	David, *you* are that man.
DAVID:	Prophet, you speak nonsense!
NATHAN:	Is not the king of Israel like a shepherd to all of his people?

DAVID:	Yes. To watch over and protect them.
NATHAN:	Did you not take and then lie with another man's wife? Bathsheba? And did you not send her husband into battle, where death was certain?
DAVID:	Oh, Lord, forgive me! What have I done?
NATHAN:	The Lord will forgive, but great suffering and humiliation will come to your house.

Scene IX: DAVID's palace, Jerusalem, 970 B.C.

LETE:	What's all the excitement about? People are filling the streets.
BOK:	Solomon, son of David and Bathsheba, has been proclaimed the new king.
LETE:	When did David die?
BOK:	He hasn't, though his time left is brief.
LETE:	I still don't understand.
BOK:	Have you forgotten David's son, Absalom, and how he conspired to overthrow his own father?
LETE:	Never will I forget how David mourned that traitor's death! I could never understand it.
BOK:	I couldn't either. At least he got what he deserved.
LETE:	Yes, snared by his own flowing hair in a tree branch.
BOK:	Until Joab skewered him with three javelins.
LETE:	I still don't understand why Solomon is king.

BOK: As David's health and strength began to fail, Adonijah began his conspiracy to become the next king. David heard of this and—

LETE: Quickly acted to guarantee his rightful succession?

BOK: Precisely. Adonijah's brief candle is out. David has charged Solomon to follow the ways of the Lord and keep the Covenant . . . .

LETE: So his reign will be great and glorious.

Life in the Ancient Western Hemisphere

Characters

SONNA, an Olmec mother   **FLAN and TEK**, Olmec temple
RAL and ONA, Olmec children   craftsmen

Scene I: Olmec home, La Venta,
Mexico, c. 900 B.C.

SONNA:	Ral, Ona, I have a very special job for you, something you've never done before.
RAL:	Yes, Mother, what is it?
SONNA:	Your father needs something to eat. I want you to take him these fresh corn cakes.
ONA:	All by ourselves?
RAL:	Why isn't he coming home to eat as he always does?
SONNA:	He's working on a very special project that must be finished before the great festival.
ONA:	When's that?
SONNA:	Come over here and I'll show you on the calendar.
ONA:	That's pretty soon. No wonder he's been working so much.
SONNA:	I also want you to give your father this message.
RAL:	What does it say?
SONNA:	Never mind. It's just between your father and me.

ONA: I sure wish we could read hieroglyphics.

RAL: This is going to be a great day. I've never been to Father's workshop before.

SONNA: It's right next to the temple, and you both know where that is. Don't stay too long. Remember, your father is under a lot of pressure with this project. Here's his food. Be careful.

Scene II: Outside temple workshops.

ONA: What do we do now? I don't know where to find Father.

                        (FLAN approaches them.)

RAL: Let's ask this man. Can you please show us where Tek works?

FLAN: I could, but he's very busy and cannot be disturbed. Run along home, now.

ONA: But we're his children and we must see him.

RAL: We've brought food and a message from our mother.

FLAN: Well, in that case . . . . Follow me.

                        (FLAN leads them inside.)

ONA: Is it far?

FLAN: Sort of. His shop is the last one in the complex.

RAL: Why's that? I thought our father did important work. Why does he have to walk so far?

FLAN: He works in the newest area, research and development.

ONA: What does that mean?

FLAN:	It's hard to explain, so I'll do it in steps . . . . Look around. What do you see?
RAL:	Workers carving huge stone heads.
ONA:	And others carving jade.
FLAN:	Correct. That's the main work here . . . all for our temples. But you're only seeing one stage of the production process.
RAL:	Please explain.
FLAN:	Well, first of all, someone must make the tools that do all the carving and shaping of stone and jade. Our research and development department has found special stones, and obsidian, a beautiful volcanic glass.
ONA:	Did our father help make the tools?
FLAN:	Yes, and he's tackled many other problems. How much do you think those stone heads weigh?
RAL:	A ton?
FLAN:	Try forty tons! Your father has been working on finding new ways to move them more easily.
ONA:	Is that what he's doing now?
FLAN:	No. He's presently working on a new product. Well, here's where your father works . . . .
	(Enter TEK, carrying two rubber balls.)
TEK:	Children, how nice to see you. But why are you here?
RAL:	We've brought you food.
ONA:	And a message from Mother.

24 Exciting Plays for Ancient History Classes

TEK: Why, thank you very much.

RAL: Father, what are you working on now?

TEK: I'm trying to make a new type of rubber ball for the upcoming games at the temple court.

ONA: Are you going to use these two?

TEK: No . . . one's too hard, and the other's too soft. *(Gives one to each child.)* I'm trying hard to develop one just in-between. Right now I'm stuck. *(Takes message and food from children.)*

RAL: So that's why you can't come home for lunch?

TEK: Right. The festival is fast approaching and the priests want this new ball ready by then. I just need to do some more experimenting.

ONA: Father, what are the big stone heads for?

TEK: *(reading his message)* They're part of our religion.

ONA: Where did our religion come from?

TEK: Our ancestors, the people who lived before us.

RAL: Who were they? Where did they come from?

TEK: Children, I have to get back to work. Ask your mother when you get home . . . and *(taking mirror from his pocket)* please give this to her.

ONA: A new polished-stone mirror! It's beautiful!

RAL: How did you know that's what mother wanted?

TEK: I read her message . . . which also said to send you two home before you started asking too many questions. Now, run along . . . and thanks for coming.

24 Exciting Plays for Ancient History Classes

Scene III: Back home, a few hours later.

ONA: Mother! We're home.

SONNA: Good. Now tell me all about your adventures while I grind this corn.

RAL: Well, we saw some workers sculpting giant stone heads.

ONA: And others carving small figures in jade.

SONNA: I'm sure you learned a lot today.

RAL: We did, but we also have many new questions.

ONA: Like who our ancestors were, and where they came from.

SONNA: Did you ask your father?

RAL: Yes, and he said to ask you . . . since you had more time.

SONNA: It figures. Well, according to the old, old stories, long ago our ancestors lived far beyond a great water.

ONA: You mean where the sun comes up in the morning?

SONNA: No, in a land far beyond where the sun sets in the evening . . . a place called Asia.

RAL: Who were they? What were they like?

SONNA: They were simple people who lived in small groups of twenty or thirty. They killed wild animals and lived off their meat, bones, and skins.

ONA: Bones? What did they use them for?

SONNA: They made sewing needles out of the small ones. The large ones were boiled and shaped into weapons.

RAL:	Did they eat corn and other vegetables, as we do?
SONNA:	No. They picked some berries, but mainly they just ate the meat they killed.
ONA:	Why did they leave the land where the sun goes down?
SONNA:	No one knows. Maybe they were searching for food, or just following the animals.
RAL:	But how did they get here? By boat?
SONNA:	They walked and walked, across the cold land where the sun hangs high in the sky all summer and only rises a little in the long dark winter. Finally, they came to a place where they could look back across the water and see the sun go down.
RAL:	That doesn't make sense. Did they cross over a great bridge?
SONNA:	Yes, and it brought them to a new land.
ONA:	But we don't live where the summer sun is always high and the winter sun is very low.
SONNA:	You're right. The people who crossed the great land-bridge long ago kept moving and moving, away from the cold and ice. After many, many years, some of them came to where we now live.
RAL:	Where we look across the great water to see the sun rising in the morning.
ONA:	Hmm. If what Mother says is right, then the land is like the rubber ball Father is making.
SONNA:	What are you talking about?
RAL:	I think she means the land must be round like a ball.

Daniel, the Prophet

Characters

LONAH, concubine
FANAS, lackey of the king
KING, Belshazzar of
  Babylonia
QUEEN

DANIEL, Hebrew captive,
  adviser to kings
MODAN, guard
CYRUS, king of Persia
VAND, **BELCO**, and **TRIG**,
  satraps (government officials)

Scene I: Palace banquet hall,
Babylon, c. 539 B.C.

LONAH:	Oh, Great King, this is the grandest, richest, and most entertaining party you've ever given.
FANAS:	I'll drink to that!
LONAH:	Belshy dear, no more wine now. Come to my chambers instead.
KING:	Later, Lonah. First, more wine.
LONAH:	No, sweetmeat. Come away before your head grows too heavy.
FANAS:	Shut up! The king wishes to drink! Stewards! More wine here!
KING:	Wait . . . let's make this a special round. Bring out the silver and gold goblets Nebuchadnezzar brought from the temple in Jerusalem years ago.
FANAS:	Yes! Yes! Fill them to overflowing!
KING:	Pass them around for all the guests to use.

FANAS:	Bottoms up, up and away!
KING:	Lonah, drink . . . drink from the captive Hebrews' sacred cup.
LONAH:	No, no. I can't . . . it's not right. I can't defile their temple goblets. I'm afraid something terrible will happen if I do.
FANAS:	What are you talking about, anyway? Why fear the captive Hebrews? They are powerless.
LONAH:	But not their God.
FANAS:	How dare you, the king's concubine, pour sour thoughts on the sweetness of his party? Your job is to give pleasure to the king, not to make him anxious with your mindless superstitions!
LONAH:	Shut up, you degenerate goat! You're nothing but a well-fed lap dog who must be told where to put his food and place his feet.
FANAS:	And you're nothing but a—
KING:	What's that?
FANAS:	What, Great King?
LONAH:	Great King, your face is whiter than ivory! Your knees are knocking. What frightens you?
KING:	Look! There's a hand writing on the wall!
FANAS:	I can't believe what I'm seeing.
KING:	What are those words? What do they mean? Fanas, assemble all the wise men here at once!
FANAS:	Immediately, Great King!

KING: And tell them that whoever can read this writing and tell
                               what it means will be richly rewarded . . . clothed in
                               purple . . . given a gold chain to wear around his neck . . .
                               and made third highest ruler in the kingdom.

Scene II: The palace, some time later.

FANAS: Great King, no one—not one of the wise men or nobles here—
                               knows what this writing means.

KING: Ayy!

                               (Enter the QUEEN.)

QUEEN: Oh, Great King, stop your wailing and worrying! There's a
                               man who can solve this mystery.

KING: Who? All of Babylon's wise men are here.

QUEEN: Not Daniel, a captive from Judah. He served King Nebuchad-
                               nezzar, your kinsman, with great distinction.

KING: Fanas, do you know of this Daniel?

FANAS: I do. He has great powers of insight and understanding. Once
                               he even told the king about a dream the king himself couldn't
                               remember!

KING: Now I recall the story . . . Nebuchadnezzar's dream about the
                               great statue with a head of gold and feet of clay. Is Daniel
                               still alive?

QUEEN: Yes, most certainly.

KING: Then have him brought here at once!

Scene III: The palace,
a short time later.

DANIEL: You want me, Great King?

KING: Are you Daniel, one of the Hebrew captives King Nebuchadnezzar brought from Judah?

DANIEL: I am.

KING: I'm told the spirit of the gods is in you, giving you great powers of wisdom and insight.

DANIEL: I am a humble servant of the one true God.

KING: If you can read that writing on the wall and tell me what it means, I'll richly reward you.

DANIEL: Keep your gifts and rewards . . . the words speak a hard and painful truth. They will give you no pleasure.

KING: Tell me! I only want to know what they say!

DANIEL: Very well. When King Nebuchadnezzar became full of his own pride and importance, the Lord God chastised him by causing his mind to snap. The king became like a simple animal, wallowing about in the grass and dew.

KING: I've heard about this craziness.

DANIEL: His sanity did not return until he acknowledged that only God is sovereign and deserves worship.

KING: That's meaningless history! What do the four words mean? I must know!

DANIEL: *Mene, Mene, Tekel, Parsin.* Since you have not humbled yourself before the Lord God, because you have shamelessly defiled His temple goblets, the days of your reign are numbered. And your kingdom will be divided amongst the Medes and Persians.

KING: Nooooooh!

(Soon after, the palace is attacked, the king is slain, and Cyrus the Persian takes over the kingdom.)

Scene IV: Royal palace, Babylon, weeks later.

MODAN:	Great King, three of your satraps are here.
CYRUS:	Send them in.
	(Enter VAND, BELCO, and TRIG.)
VAND:	Great King and conqueror—
BELCO:	We stand ready to serve—
TRIG:	And make your empire greater each day.
CYRUS:	Good . . . that's why I've called you here. Presently, the realm is administered by three men: Vand, Belco, and Daniel.
VAND:	Is there something wrong with this arrangement?
BELCO:	Are we not doing our jobs?
CYRUS:	You are. I want Trig to take over Daniel's position.
TRIG:	Thank you for your confidence in me.
VAND:	But what about Daniel?
CYRUS:	I've created a new position for him. You three will now be under his authority.
BELCO:	What? And Daniel just below you, the king? He's but a captive, an alien from Judah.
CYRUS:	I couldn't care less where he comes from. He's already shown his worth ten times over! The man has brains, wisdom, and integrity. You can't corrupt him! Now, see to it that all the other officials are notified of this change.

24 Exciting Plays for Ancient History Classes

VAND:	Hmmm. Great King, please allow one suggestion.
CYRUS:	I'm listening.
VAND:	It is true that Daniel is a capable administrator. But this promotion, this exalted position, might not be accepted by the others . . . and . . . .
CYRUS:	Because he's not of our race? I told you, I don't care about that. Besides, his race has not been an issue before.
BELCO:	Race is not the issue. Authority is. If the lower officials question Daniel's new power, yours as king will be weakened.
CYRUS:	What do you suggest I do?
TRIG:	Have your absolute power and authority reconfirmed.
BELCO:	Yes—to maintain unity throughout the empire, and head off feelings of jealousy and envy resulting from Daniel's elevation.
VAND:	Otherwise, intrigue will spread like a cancer—
TRIG:	Leading to subversion and outright rebellion!
CYRUS:	I see. So you think it's necessary that all my subjects pledge their loyalty to me?
BELCO:	More than pledge . . . worship! That will be a more useful test for safeguarding your authority.
VAND:	I've quickly written an appropriate edict: "Anyone who prays to any god or man, except to the king, during the next thirty days, shall be thrown into the lions' den."
TRIG:	Just sign it, and we'll make sure it's enforced.
CYRUS:	Very well. Here's my royal seal.

Scene V: Royal palace, days later.

MODAN: Great King, three of your chief administrators await your presence.

(Enter the three.)

VAND: Great King, did you not recently sign a decree stating that anyone who did not pray to you would be thrown into the lions' den?

CYRUS: Yes. You three thought it politically expedient.

BELCO: And according to the law of the Medes and Persians, no decree issued by the king can be changed?

TRIG: Even by the king himself?

CYRUS: Of course . . . you know very well that once it's written down . . . . Say, where's all this going?

VAND: One of your officials has not complied.

BELCO: Three times a day, in his chambers, he prays to the Hebrew God.

TRIG: Your exalted servant, Daniel.

VAND: Many already know of his disloyalty.

CYRUS: Let me guess who spread the news.

BELCO: You must promptly enforce your edict, or your authority throughout the empire will be severely compromised.

CYRUS: Modan, bring Daniel here. You three certainly have spun a crafty web . . . maybe too crafty.

Scene VI: Outside the lions' den, that night.

DANIEL: Great King, I have never been disloyal to you. Do not be alarmed. God knows my heart.

CYRUS: I am sick with anger and depression for what I've done. May your God rescue you!

(Daniel enters the lions' den.)

Scene VII: Outside the lions' den, the next morning.

MODAN: Great King, shall I remove the covering stone?

CYRUS: Yes, immediately! . . . Daniel, Daniel! Has your God preserved you?

MODAN: Great King, please do not trouble your heart with impossible hopes. The lions were kept without food for days. It will be a gory sight I wish to spare you from seeing.

DANIEL: *(calling from inside den)* Great King, my God sent an angel to shut the mouths of the lions.

CYRUS: Daniel lives! Modan! Lift him out at once! Praise be to your God!

MODAN: *(helping Daniel out of den)* I can't believe this. I can't believe this.

CYRUS: Modan, I will issue a decree that throughout my kingdom all people must fear and revere the God of Daniel.

MODAN: Shall I give this order to Vand, Belco, and Trig?

CYRUS: No, to their immediate subordinates. Throw those three into the lions' den!

The Buddha and the Five Visitors

Characters

STUDENT   **PAINSOUL**   **CIVICSOUL**
BUDDHA   **FORMSOUL**   **MEANSOUL**
GUTSOUL

Scene I: A garden retreat, India, c. 485 B.C.

STUDENT: Enlightened One, a small caravan has stopped nearby. I see five men.

BUDDHA: Welcome them all. Ask them their needs.

(STUDENT exits and returns with the five.)

STUDENT: They seek only cool water, a warm fire, and shelter for the night.

BUDDHA: Nothing else?

GUTSOUL: Plenty more! I could do with a great feast, a wine cup that's never empty, and some beautiful dancing girls.

BUDDHA: Is that truly your heart's desire?

GUTSOUL: Of course! Why else does a man live? Why do I take great effort and pain to reach the great city? Because there I can make the money to buy all my desires.

BUDDHA: I once lived the life of a rich prince.

GUTSOUL: Excellent! Then we understand each other. Wealth and pleasure . . . the only life worth striving for.

BUDDHA:	But such striving never ends. You satisfy your physical senses only to fall asleep. When you awake, you must again rush here and there to fill your pleasure. First comes exhaustion, and then, sooner or later, cynicism. You're only keeping a candle lit in a dark and windy cave.
PAINSOUL:	I do not strive to please the senses. I seek spiritual fulfillment.
STUDENT:	And how do you seek it?
PAINSOUL:	Through great physical pain and suffering.
BUDDHA:	I once lived like that. Seeds and grass, even dung, were my food. I wore hair cloth, stood still for long hours, lay upon thorns, and did not bathe so I looked like an old tree. I even slept among rotting carcasses.
PAINSOUL:	Did this not bring you to a higher spiritual level?
BUDDHA:	No. It only brought me a foolish pride.
FORMSOUL:	The higher plane can only be reached by performing the rituals.
STUDENT:	Rituals of what?
FORMSOUL:	The true religion. That is my journey's purpose. I am going to the holy city to perform the proper rituals.
BUDDHA:	And if along the way you pass through a desert and meet a blind man seeking water, what will you do?
FORMSOUL:	If I have enough water, I will share some with him.
STUDENT:	And if you do not have enough, will you help him find some?
FORMSOUL:	Of course, if I am near my destination.
BUDDHA:	And if you are far from it?

FORMSOUL:	I will ask someone else to assist him. He will understand that I must hurry to the holy place.
CIVICSOUL:	Hypocrite! What kind of religion is that? Religion should build sincerity, not selfish convenience. Sincerity is the cornerstone of character.
STUDENT:	Tell us more.
CIVICSOUL:	I come from China. There I learned the ideas of Confucius, ideas to improve and strengthen our communities.
STUDENT:	And how is this done?
CIVICSOUL:	By raising up leaders who are noble, honest, and incorruptible.
STUDENT:	Certainly. But where do you find such leaders? I think you are a dreamer.
CIVICSOUL:	No laws can create them. Only noble families can.
STUDENT:	Please explain.
CIVICSOUL:	No family can function nobly without order and control.
STUDENT:	What do you mean?
CIVICSOUL:	Where there is order . . . sincerity, justice, goodness, and harmony bloom as petals in the family flower.
STUDENT:	What about the individual?
CIVICSOUL:	I'm pleased you asked. A well-ordered family can only be made from disciplined and ordered individuals.
STUDENT:	Which brings us full circle to noble leaders.
CIVICSOUL:	Yes. Their noble lives inspire and guide the people to justice and harmony.

MEANSOUL:	Enough of this mindless raving! Pompous and stupid baboons, all of you. Especially you—the one they call Enlightened.
STUDENT:	Please tame your beastly tongue, traveler.
BUDDHA:	Let him speak.
MEANSOUL:	And I suppose I'm to feel gratitude? Ha! As I was about to say, "Enlightened One," your speech is but foul-smelling air, your wisdom reeks like fresh dung.
BUDDHA:	I teach my disciples to return evil with kindness.
MEANSOUL:	Don't play word games with me, old man. I spit on your sappy kindness. It's worse than dog vomit to me.
STUDENT:	Enlightened One, you need not take such mindless abuse. Let me take him away.
BUDDHA:	Wait. I have but one short question for him.
MEANSOUL:	Go ahead, drivel-mouth.
BUDDHA:	Friend, if someone offers you a gift and you do not accept it, who is its owner?
MEANSOUL:	Owner of the gift? Why, the one who offered it.
BUDDHA:	Very well. Now, since I will not accept the abuse you offer, keep it to yourself, and go in peace.

Ancient Athens: Citizen Debate

Characters

STATQUOS   **PHILOS**   **SPARTOS**
RADICOS   **YUPPOS**

Scene I: Citizens' assembly, Athens, Greece, 440 B.C.

STATQUOS: Citizens, the issue needing attention is both critical and mundane—money. For over seven years the Parthenon has been under construction—

RADICOS: Seven wasted years if you ask me. Let us discuss more urgent matters.

PHILOS: This is a priority for Athens. Continue.

STATQUOS: Thank you. The project should be completed within three years.

YUPPOS: That long? What's the hang-up?

STATQUOS: As a temple worthy of our great city and our patron goddess, Athena Parthenos, it requires more funds for additional materials.

SPARTOS: I have spent many early mornings jogging around the site. The architecture is heroic, the craftsmanship superb. But the appropriate statues are missing.

STATQUOS: Precisely . . . and marble means money.

RADICOS: Ha! The truth is, that greedy architect Ictinus and that fumbling sculptor Phidias are milking the public treasury dry. They're playing us all for suckers.

STATQUOS: Ridiculous! Those two are the finest men in their respective fields. They are dedicated public servants and citizens. They care nothing for personal wealth.

RADICOS: How about personal artistic immortality? No expense has been spared feeding their glory . . . and his.

YUPPOS: His? Are you cynically referring to Pericles?

RADICOS: Very perceptive, Yuppos. It seems your brain can function beyond sneaky business deals.

PHILOS: Citizens, you are both off the mark. The Parthenon is not the glory of our leader . . . or even of our artists and craftsmen. It is a symbol of Athens, our collective spirit in stone, a sublime statement of who we are and what we're about . . . .

YUPPOS: Honeyed sentiments to attract our hard-earned money for supporting fat-bottomed bureaucrats!

STATQUOS: Could our city's wealth be spent more nobly?

YUPPOS: From your point of view, no. But the real question is why so much private wealth is spent on public projects.

PHILOS: It is our heritage. We Athenians are public people. We do not live behind closed doors to pursue only private interests and entertainments.

STATQUOS: As citizens we have freely decided how to use our wealth.

YUPPOS: Sure . . . and I'm Sophocles or Socrates, take your pick. If we truly are a free and democratic society, I would like to freely choose to keep *my* wealth to *my*self! Ah . . . look at Corinth . . . what luxurious living!

SPARTOS: *(giving YUPPOS a card)* Here's a little card for you.

YUPPOS: *(reading)* "Athens—love it or leave it." Very funny, barbell-brain.

STATQUOS: Would you have Athens spend no money for public buildings? What would happen to our temples, theaters, and gymnasiums?

YUPPOS: I'm not against them. It's just that I believe each project or activity should pay for itself. If it can't, then let it die quietly.

RADICOS: What you're really asking is that religion, drama, sports, and fitness be only for the rich.

YUPPOS: If people want something badly enough, they'll pay the price. Isn't that being democratic?

PHILOS: You would have Athens degenerate into a frenzied, money-chasing market of competing interests. What energies would remain for our citizens to reflect, debate, develop art, exercise, and cultivate honest friendships?

YUPPOS: If Athens continues her present course, the "public life" you idealize will wither and die.

STATQUOS: Ridiculous! You don't make any sense.

YUPPOS: Oh? Don't you realize that more and more of our wealth is based on the labor of slaves and the enterprise of foreigners? Losing economic control will ultimately cost us our political and cultural independence.

SPARTOS: He has a point. We *are* losing control of our society, but not for economic reasons.

PHILOS: What reasons, then?

SPARTOS: Look at our youth: their wills are self-centered, their bodies soft and flabby.

STATQUOS: You're exaggerating! We always perform well at the Olympic Games. Look at our glorious gymnasiums.

SPARTOS: Built purely for pleasure. We lack *discipline*, the discipline that does not flinch at pain or coddle to mushy sentiment!

PHILOS:	And how would you arrest this decay and weakness?
SPARTOS:	Take all well-bodied boys out of the home at age seven. Place them in army camps. Give them the severest physical training. Teach them to fight and obey. Keep them in the army for life. Let slaves produce the food.
PHILOS:	That's how the Spartans live! An artless tyranny controlled by an immoral pack of obedient and well-fed fighting dogs.
STATQUOS:	Well and truly stated, Philos. Now, since when were Athenians poor fighters? Did we not defeat the mighty Persians?
SPARTOS:	With Sparta's brave and generous support.
STATQUOS:	Agreed.
PHILOS:	But Athens fought for more than mere survival. We battled and bled to preserve our heritage, our civic ideals.
STATQUOS:	Yes—the steadfast rule of law, as Solon formulated, and not the rule of shifting passions.
PHILOS:	And the rights of all citizens as first guaranteed by Cleisthenes.
RADICOS:	*All* citizens? Oh, come now. You mock logic. Are women citizens? And slaves?
STATQUOS:	What are you talking about? Women have their place in Athens—in the home. Our slaves are well treated. So, what's your point?
RADICOS:	A simple and unsettling one. Until slavery is abolished, and women can go about public business as we do, our so-called democracy is a sham. It will degenerate and die.
PHILOS:	Nonsense! Athens was never stronger. Look at our formidable army, and our growing naval power. We are a vibrant society. Foreigners marvel at our drama, architecture, and sports.

24 Exciting Plays for Ancient History Classes

STATQUOS: And above all, Athens is strong because its citizens believe rationally in its principles and values.

PHILOS: Unlike Sparta, which commands only blind obedience, or Persia, with its feverish and shifting emotionalism.

RADICOS: You are both wrong. The so-called unity of belief and support you claim for Athens is but an empty shell. Too many Athenians are excluded from public life and power. The core of Athens' strength is hollow. Grand buildings like the Parthenon cannot fill it. Neither can the glories and conquests of war.

YUPPOS: What can rebuild that vital core?

RADICOS: Universal citizenship.

STATQUOS: That would not be Athens.

RADICOS: Heed my words. Out of our disunity will come many wars, wars that will drain our strength and sap our spirit. Eventually we will be conquered, and the conquerors will spread far and wide the ideals and culture of an Athens that once was . . . .

Ancient Greece: 432-399 B.C.

Characters

ANDROS, a Greek citizen
  and farmer
ZENOS, son of Andros
ALEXIS, son of Andros
DIDRA, wife of Andros

CASSIE, daughter of Andros
HOMER, a slave
RASION, a merchant and
  "metic"
ZORA, wife of Rasion

Scene I: Country olive farm, Greece,
c. 432 B.C.

ANDROS: Zenos, come down and get your younger brother.

ZENOS: Can't it wait? I've almost finished picking this tree.

ANDROS: No, it can't.

ALEXIS: Father, what's all the fuss about? We have loads of work to do.

ANDROS: I know, I know. Once your mother and sister arrive, we're going to have a family meeting.

(Enter DIDRA and CASSIE with food and drink.)

DIDRA: Here's some refreshment for the hard workers.

ANDROS: I have something very important to announce . . . . I'm sending Alexis to Athens to learn the overseas trading business.

DIDRA: Is the sun playing tricks with your brain? We're Greek citizens, above such crude pursuits as haggling and trading. Only metics are merchants.

ANDROS:	The times are changing.
ZENOS:	Father, excuse me . . . but this makes absolutely no sense. We can't run this farm without Alexis.
DIDRA:	He's right. We're not like the idle fountain-mouthed citizens of Athens—
ZENOS:	Who spend all their waking hours arguing politics and running after "truth" and "beauty"—
DIDRA:	Or watching silly plays and games—
ZENOS:	While letting the slaves and foreigners do all the work!
CASSIE:	Don't forget the women and girls!
ALEXIS:	Face it, little sister, Greece is a man's world.
ANDROS:	Hold it! We're way off the subject. Of course we need Alexis here. Athenians depend on every olive we pick to make their cooking oil and lamp fuel.
DIDRA:	Then why are you sending Alexis there? We poor country Greeks are consumed by curiosity!
ANDROS:	I fear that war is coming to Athens and all Attica.
CASSIE:	Against whom?
ANDROS:	Sparta.
ZENOS:	What? But we were allies in driving out the Persians.
ANDROS:	That was many years ago.
ALEXIS:	What do they want from us?
ANDROS:	Come, come now. Our rich silver mines, for one. And they hate Athens for the way it dominates the Peloponnesian League and treasury.

ZENOS:	But if war does come, why have Alexis in Athens?
ANDROS:	Do you realize what the Spartans will do to our olive orchards if they get here?
ZENOS:	Destroy them as the Persians once did.
ANDROS:	Precisely. And where would that leave us? Or have you forgotten how long it takes us to bring a new olive tree to maturity?
CASSIE:	Sixteen years. Isn't that what you said, Father?
ANDROS:	To bear fruit, yes. Forty years to maturity.
DIDRA:	So you're hoping Alexis will earn a fortune in foreign trade?
ANDROS:	Yes . . . our insurance if the worst comes.
CASSIE:	Can I go with Alexis? Please, please! I want to see all those beautiful buildings, all those silly plays and games. I want to shop and shop at the agora until I can't stand up. I want to talk politics and art, too.
DIDRA:	Daughter, have you forgotten what Alexis said? It's a man's world out there. In Athens girls can't go to those places. Women can't even go shopping!
ANDROS:	Your mother's right, Cassie. Females live very secluded lives in Athens.
ALEXIS:	So appreciate your freedom out here in the countryside.
ANDROS:	Alexis, here's a letter of introduction to the merchant shipper Rasion. He's a metic.
CASSIE:	Father, what are metics? Are they slaves?
ANDROS:	No, free men. But since they're foreign born, they are not considered citizens.

24 Exciting Plays for Ancient History Classes

ZENOS:	Which means they can't vote in the assembly. But without them, Athens wouldn't have much of an economy.
ANDROS:	Or international flavor . . . Athens would be just another narrow-minded Greek backwater.

Scene II: Merchant's home, Athens, a week later.

HOMER:	What can I do for you, young man?
ALEXIS:	I have a letter of introduction for Rasion, the merchant shipper.
HOMER:	Master, a young man from the countryside has a letter for you.
RASION:	Let him in . . . I'm expecting him.
HOMER:	Shall I bring some refreshment . . . wash his feet?
RASION:	Not now, we'll soon be leaving. You must be Alexis, son of Andros.
ALEXIS:	Yes. I am most grateful for your time.
RASION:	And I am most grateful for your father's business. He sends me the finest olives, and never tries to cheat me . . . unlike most of the vendors down at the agora.
ALEXIS:	We country people are like that.
RASION:	Well, city people sure aren't. They'll try anything and everything to get the advantage. No scruples whatsoever! And another thing I like about your father . . . he treats me with respect. Most Greek citizens look down their noses at metics.
ALEXIS:	He respects anyone who does honest work and isn't afraid to sweat and get dirty.

RASION:	A rare sentiment. Most Greeks only get dirty and sweaty in their gymnasiums!
ALEXIS:	What do you mean?
RASION:	Oh. Gymnasiums are places where they exercise, box, wrestle, and even train for the Olympics.
ALEXIS:	I got plenty of exercise on the farm.
RASION:	I bet you did. You have to understand, these Greeks worship perfection: body, mind, and soul. That's why they have such elaborate gymnasiums, numerous places for talk, and beautiful temples.
ALEXIS:	Which you don't frequent because you're too busy making a living.
RASION:	Somebody has to keep this ship afloat.
ALEXIS:	But aren't you angry over your lack of political power?
RASION:	Just because we metics can't vote doesn't mean we're without influence. Besides, there are laws which protect us, and Athens is still the biggest grape, if you know what I mean.

(Enter ZORA.)

ZORA:	And who is our guest, dear husband?
RASION:	Zora, my love . . . this is Alexis. He's going to work for me.
ALEXIS:	I'm pleased to meet you. Excuse me, but I thought city women were secluded from male visitors.
RASION:	And were kept in a back room carding wool and pressing olives?
ALEXIS:	Yes . . . something like that.

RASION:	Not in this household. Most Greek men marry girls half their age and only care about the dowries they bring. Me, I married Zora for love. She's from Egypt.
ZORA:	I brought no dowry, only affection for Rasion.
RASION:	I wanted a true partner and companion, not some empty-headed girl who spends her time trying to be like these Greeks! She's also a great help in the business.
ALEXIS:	Do you have any children?
ZORA:	Only little Agnes. She was born with a deformed leg so she has trouble walking.
RASION:	Our precious little flower. You're surprised she still lives with us . . . and that we didn't expose her as a newborn to the cruel elements? Like the "good" citizens of Athens do with their weak and infirm babies? Never!
ZORA:	That's the dark side of the Greeks' drive for perfection. We may be practical-minded merchants, but we're also people of great sentiment and feeling, especially for the weak and defenseless.
RASION:	Unlike the high-minded Greeks . . . . Enough of this heavy conversation. Let's head for Piraeus and see some of my ships!
ALEXIS:	Is it far? I've already walked some distance.
RASION:	Less than ten kilometers. You'll find the roadway most unusual.
ALEXIS:	Why's that?
RASION:	It has protective walls on both sides, all along the route.
ALEXIS:	For what purpose?
RASION:	In case of war, Athens will not be cut off from food and supplies.

ZORA:	Like when the Persians burned the city years ago.
ALEXIS:	Who came up with the idea?
RASION:	Pericles, leader of Athens.

Scene III: Country olive farm, c. 399 B.C.

CASSIE:	Who goes there? If you're a Spartan, don't bother. There's nothing left.
ALEXIS:	I am Alexis, son of Andros, gone for thirty years.
CASSIE:	Alexis, brother to Cassie?
ALEXIS:	Yes! And brother to Zenos and son of Didra!
CASSIE:	My brother! We've waited so long, and suffered so dearly . . . only your brother and I are left.
ALEXIS:	Where is Zenos?
CASSIE:	In the house, resting. He nearly died in the war. Look about and see what the Spartans did.
ALEXIS:	The orchards are all gone . . . I'm so sorry I wasn't here to help. Oh, that blasted Peloponnesian War . . . I couldn't get back. But I have plenty of money now to care for you both.
CASSIE:	Thank you. But what's important is . . . you didn't forget. You didn't forget your family and ideals. The rest of Greece has.
ALEXIS:	I know. It's as if Greece has committed suicide.
CASSIE:	How are things where you came from?

24 Exciting Plays for Ancient History Classes

ALEXIS:	Very bad. After Sparta humiliated Athens, Athens began turning on itself.
CASSIE:	What do you mean?
ALEXIS:	They just executed a great man.
CASSIE:	Why?
ALEXIS:	For his ideas.
CASSIE:	*What?* A Greek put to death for his *thoughts*? I can't believe it. What was his name?
ALEXIS:	Socrates.

24 Exciting Plays for Ancient History Classes

Alexander the Great: Dream to the Winds

Scene I: Royal court, Pella, Macedonia, 349 B.C.

OLYMPIAS: Alexander, now that you are seven, and no longer a child, it's time for you to systematically prepare for your destiny.

ALEXANDER: Yes, Mother.

OLYMPIAS: My uncle, Leonidas, will be your tutor. He is ready to begin.

(Exit OLYMPIAS, enter LEONIDAS.)

LEONIDAS: Alexander, what do you think I'll try to teach you?

ALEXANDER: How to become a great warrior and king like my father.

LEONIDAS: Hmmm. How do the artisans make your father's spears so hard?

ALEXANDER: By putting them into a very hot fire.

LEONIDAS: Yes. And that's how you will become strong and able.

ALEXANDER:	Will you try to put me into a fire?
LEONIDAS:	In a way . . . through the flames of discipline: lean diet, hard exercise, sleep on the ground, and marches in the middle of the night.
ALEXANDER:	Why that way?
LEONIDAS:	Alexander, a man cannot lead unless he first commands his own body and spirit. No more can you live the soft, flabby, and lazy life.

Scene II: Royal court, Pella, Macedonia, a year later.

PHILIP:	Alexander, is that you singing?
ALEXANDER:	Yes, my father.
PHILIP:	Shame! Shame for a warrior's son to sing so sweetly, like a girl.
OLYMPIAS:	How cruel of you!
PHILIP:	Shut up, Olympias. I know what makes a king.
OLYMPIAS:	Ha! You know only treachery and lust, the meat and marrow of your reign. The gods have written for Alexander a different script.
	(Exit PHILIP.)
ALEXANDER:	Mother, what are you talking about?
OLYMPIAS:	Your father is a strong warrior, as you shall one day be. But always remember that you come from the seed of Achilles.
ALEXANDER:	Yes, Mother.

24 Exciting Plays for Ancient History Classes

OLYMPIAS:	Your father is sometimes a careless and insensitive fool . . . . Know that your destiny is to soar far above all mortals like him . . . upon the wings of your will and spirit.

Scene III: Royal stables, 343 *B.C.*

ANTER:	Sire, it's no use. The steed will not be broken. All my men have failed.
PHILIP:	What a pity . . . such a noble and spirited horse to roam only in the shadows of glory. Send Bucephalus back.
ALEXANDER:	Father, wait! Let me try!
PHILIP:	Nonsense! You're too frail, and only thirteen . . . Alexander! Stop!
ANTER:	I can't believe my eyes! How did the boy do it?
PHILIP:	Well done, my son! Bucephalus is yours. Ride him to glory!
ANTER:	Alexander, how did you calm him?
ALEXANDER:	I observed that Bucephalus bolted only when he saw his own shadow. I simply faced him to the sun, mounted, and kept his head up.

Scene IV: Royal court, Pella, Macedonia, 342 *B.C.*

PHILIP:	Alexander, meet your new tutor, Aristotle. His father was court physician to my father.
	(Exit PHILIP, enter ARISTOTLE.)
ALEXANDER:	You are Greek?
ARISTOTLE:	Yes . . . from Athens.
ALEXANDER:	My father admires Greek culture, but distrusts your politics.

ARISTOTLE:	Oh . . . Alexander, what is your life's goal?
ALEXANDER:	My destiny—to rule the world.
ARISTOTLE:	For what purpose?
ALEXANDER:	To gain immortal glory.
ARISTOTLE:	And what is that glory? Is it to see your royal banner flying above the Persians' palace?
ALEXANDER:	Yes, yes.
ARISTOTLE:	And above every mud and straw hut whose inhabitants live desperate lives, like helpless, driven beasts?
ALEXANDER:	You Greeks are clever. Where are you leading me?
ARISTOTLE:	To understand true glory.
ALEXANDER:	Go on . . . .
ARISTOTLE:	After the sword of victory, bring to the conquered people the light of Greek civilization: her literature, philosophy, science, and art.
ALEXANDER:	Yes! I will not only conquer, but create—create a new world. Now you must begin to fill my cup with your knowledge.
ARISTOTLE:	Even ideas concerning *how* to conquer?
ALEXANDER:	That won't be necessary. I've learned well from my father.
ARISTOTLE:	I'm sure you have . . . but a man should never stop learning, even in warfare. Some battles require the brawn of a bear, some the engineering of a beaver, some the speed of a deer— and all battles require the cunning of a fox.
ALEXANDER:	Why do you use animals in your counsel?

ARISTOTLE:	Because nature is our greatest teacher. Observe, Alexander. Always observe. Then use logic to give meaning to your experiences. The mind is a person's greatest power. Foolish people only react. The great-souled person first dreams, then creates and shapes events to fulfill these dreams.
ALEXANDER:	I wish to be such a man, a great leader.
ARISTOTLE:	Then you must shape the wills and spirits of your followers.
ALEXANDER:	Why? Isn't giving orders enough?
ARISTOTLE:	No. You must lead by your own brave example. You must own and share every soldier's danger, discomfort, and deprivation. If you do, your troops will follow any plan, to any place.
ALEXANDER:	I understand . . . I only hope my father leaves me something to conquer.

Scene V: Gordium, Asia Minor, 333 *B.C.*

HEPHAESTION:	We're approaching the legendary Gordian Knot. No mortal man has yet mastered its strength or complexity. Alexander, will you give it a go?
CRATERUS:	All you have to do is untie it to release the wagon.
PTOLEMY:	I think Alexander will do it his own way.
	(ALEXANDER cuts the knot with one stroke of his sword.)
HEPHAESTION:	Behold! The Gordian Knot is no more!

Scene VI: Port of Tyre (Lebanon) 332 *B.C.*

PARMENION:	Oh, King, the Tyrians have murdered our emissaries and thrown their bodies into the sea.

ALEXANDER:	What treachery!
PARMENION:	The humane way you treated the captured Persian royal household at Issus makes no mark with these barbarians.
NEARCHUS:	The fort must be secured. Otherwise the Persian fleet will use it as a base to destroy our communications.
ALEXANDER:	But if we take it, the Persian fleet will have no port for supplies.
NEARCHUS:	And ultimately be forced to surrender.
PARMENION:	But the cost! A half mile of water separates us. The fort's walls are over one hundred feet high! We need more fire-power. Our ships will be like sitting ducks.
ALEXANDER:	Bring Aristobulus, the engineer, at once.
NEARCHUS:	Tell us your thoughts, my King.
ALEXANDER:	Consider the patient beaver . . . . We will build a causeway out to their island fort. Nearchus, gather every ship in Phoenicia. By land and sea we'll lay siege to Tyre.

Scene VII: Alexander's headquarters, Tyre, seven months later.

NEARCHUS:	Alexander, the walls are crumbling! Our catapults and battering rams have succeeded!
PARMENION:	And our forces have landed.
	(PERSIAN MESSENGER arrives and gives ALEXANDER a message.)
ALEXANDER:	*(reading)* Very interesting. Darius wants a peace treaty. He knows Tyre will soon be ours.
NEARCHUS:	What are the Persian's terms?

ALEXANDER: He offers us ten thousand talents in gold, his daughter in marriage, and all territory west of the Euphrates . . . .

NEARCHUS: That's one third of the whole Persian Empire!

PARMENION: If I were king, I'd accept.

ALEXANDER: And if I were Parmenion, so would I. No negotiations! After Tyre, on to Egypt. Then east, past the ends of all Persia!

Scene VIII: Alexander's camp, Beas River, India, 326 B.C.

PTOLEMY: The troops are growing increasingly restless.

CRATERUS: The recent hard fighting against King Porus and his elephants has unnerved many.

HEPHAESTION: The death of Cleitus by Alexander's own hand has alienated many of the Macedonian troops.

CRATERUS: Why did he do it? Cleitus saved Alexander's very life at Granicus.

PTOLEMY: It was the bitter fruit of a drunken rage. Cleitus had no business speaking as he did.

CRATERUS: What? Telling the king he was becoming too Persian? That too many former enemies were appointed officers and governors? Has he forgotten his roots?

HEPHAESTION: Have you forgotten his dream? Alexander wanted to unite all peoples into a great civilization.

CRATERUS: The men are tired of dreams. They're sick of the constant rain, bad food, and snakes. They're weary from marching across scorching deserts and frozen mountain passes.

HEPHAESTION: But hasn't Alexander shared all this, too?

CRATERUS: Yes, as always. But we, and especially Alexander, must face facts. The men will go no further. They miss their families.

PTOLEMY:	You are right, and he must be told. Alexander's own troops will give him his only defeat.

Scene IX: Public square, Babylon, 323 B.C.

MATTON:	Binas, old comrade in arms. Sit with me for a while.
BINAS:	Yes. Let us grieve Alexander's death together.
MATTON:	You were with him from the beginning. How will you remember him? How he conquered the whole world?
BINAS:	No. His empire will break apart before long. I'll recall how he outfoxed old Darius at Gaugamela.
MATTON:	And finished off the Persian empire.
BINAS:	Remember how he made us all get a good night's rest while Darius made his men stand watch the whole night and grow weary?
MATTON:	And how we crushed their chariots the next day!
BINAS:	Yes. Instead of attacking head on, Alexander had us wait, and then part to let the Persians race through.
MATTON:	While they fumbled with their chariots to turn around, we gave them our heavy metal.
BINAS:	And what will you remember about him?
MATTON:	The time in India when he went out on a very dangerous mission. He took an arrow to his lung. I'll never forget how he fought to survive.
BINAS:	He was a fighter, all right, and he always suffered right along with us.

24 Exciting Plays for Ancient History Classes

MATTON:	That's it! He was always part of us. He even knew my name.
BINAS:	Mine, too! He was always talking with the foot soldiers.
MATTON:	Yes . . . but what I'll most remember is when we were finally coming home. We were in the desert and the heat was unbearable. There wasn't any water left. I found a small puddle, only enough to fill my helmet, and brought it to Alexander. Remember what he did as we all watched?
BINAS:	Yes. He threw the water to the winds, and we all cheered.

Asoka and the Mauryan Empire (India)

Characters

SAYHA and DRAN, Mauryan officials	**ASOKA**, king
CHUNG, a Chinese traveler	**GARL**, a messenger
JAILER	**BOYA**, a Buddhist teacher
SERINE, a Buddhist	**VIZIER**, chief minister
AIDE (to the King)	**FAYNG**, an army general

Scene I: Hotel, Ujjain, Mauryan Empire, c. 265 B.C.

SAYHA: Well, my friend, are you ready for the long journey home?

DRAN: Yes. I just finished my last appointment.

SAYHA: Would you mind another traveling companion?

DRAN: I saw no other officials here from the capital.

SAYHA: He's Chinese.

DRAN: A foreigner? No way. We're still on official government business.

SAYHA: Are you worried, by chance, about spies?

DRAN: Of course. The king has them everywhere. That's how he keeps control over this vast empire.

SAYHA: You're paranoid.

DRAN: You know the regulations. *No exceptions.* I don't want to lose this job—or my good health.

SAYHA: You won't. I just want to relieve the tedium of the trip. If anyone asks, I'll say our guest is from his country's ministry of transportation.

DRAN: Oh . . . all right.

(SAYHA beckons to CHUNG, who enters.)

SAYHA: Good, now let's all mount our beast. Chung, this is Dran. He works for the Empire's department of navigation. And as you recall I'm in communications.

CHUNG: Yes. Thank you very much. I've never ridden an elephant before.

SAYHA: One of the perks of our government positions. Otherwise, only the nobility uses them.

CHUNG: I've traveled mainly on your rivers. What an extensive water network! I found them very safe and efficient, especially the ferries.

SAYHA: That's Dran's doing. His people are very competent.

DRAN: For the next few days you'll experience the fruits of Sayha's department.

CHUNG: You mean this wide and well-maintained road?

SAYHA: Yes. An extensive and well-run infrastructure is a top priority. Our roads and waterways tie the Empire together—

DRAN: Stimulating trade and streamlining communications.

CHUNG: That's certain. How did this all come about?

SAYHA: Sixty or so years ago Alexander, the Macedonian, invaded India.

DRAN: We are told he had much success until he met a united opposition.

SAYHA: His own generals forced him to retreat.

DRAN: Seven years later, Chandragupta Maurya drove out the remaining Macedonians.

SAYHA: He created the Mauryan Empire. His grandson, Asoka, is now our king.

CHUNG: What was the old Chandragupta like?

DRAN: A brave and brilliant warrior, and a shrewd king.

CHUNG: In what ways?

SAYHA: He carefully selected advisors and officials with great administrative ability.

DRAN: He also organized every aspect of the political, economic, and cultural life of the Empire under the authority of some department.

SAYHA: And he had an invisible network of spies and informers to keep order and control.

CHUNG: What about those who didn't abide by the system?

DRAN: Punishment, swift and severe! Sometimes torture, sometimes even mutilation.

CHUNG: I have traveled many weeks in your kingdom. Even the lowliest day laborers seem well fed and content.

SAYHA: The government diligently conserves food. During a famine it distributes the surplus to everyone. The government also provides hospitals and promotes sanitation.

CHUNG: But I've also seen a very rigid social caste system. Can anyone change his position?

DRAN: No, no one can change position. But have you seen any slaves?

SAYHA:	In India we have a saying, "Each has a role, all have a place."
CHUNG:	Speaking of places, what's your capital like?
DRAN:	Pataliputra? It's nine miles long and nearly two miles wide. The pillars of the royal palace are plated with gold.
CHUNG:	And Taxila? That's where I'm going . . . to study.
SAYHA:	A wonderful and stimulating town, home of our greatest university. Students from all over the Orient study at the medical school there.
CHUNG:	Splendid! Say, what's the present king like?
SAYHA:	Asoka? Just like his grandfather . . . a hard and driven man.
DRAN:	So true. But I've also heard he has a bit of the dreamer in him.

Scene II: Dungeon, outside capital.

JAILER:	Ah . . . the religious fanatic. What statute of the Mauryan Empire did you violate?
SERINE:	None. I seek only truth and peace.
JAILER:	Isn't that nice . . . I seek only comfort and warmth for my charges. Into the royal hot tub.
	(SERINE is tied and placed into a cauldron which the JAILER soon brings to a boil.)
	What are you smiling about? Hey! What's wrong? How come nothing's happening? The king should know about this.

Scene III: Royal palace, Pataliputra, a short time later.

AIDE:	King Asoka, a messenger from your dungeon.

24 Exciting Plays for Ancient History Classes

ASOKA: Bring him in.

                    (GARL enters.)

GARL: Great King, something unbelievable is happening at the
                    royal dungeon!

ASOKA: All I care about is my orders being obeyed!

GARL: I know . . . that's what the jailer did. He placed a religious
                    prisoner into the cauldron . . . .

ASOKA: And? Spit it out, man! I'm very busy!

GARL: The man's flesh would not boil!

ASOKA: Obviously the fire was not properly prepared.

GARL: But it was! Come see for yourself.

ASOKA: Very well. I need a diversion.

Scene IV: Royal dungeon, a few minutes later.

JAILER: Now do you believe?

ASOKA: I have seen the impossible! Who is this man?

JAILER: A Buddhist holy man. What should I do with him?

ASOKA: Take him out, idiot! I'll deal with him later. But I must return
                    now to the palace.

JAILER: Oh, King, have you forgotten your immutable edict?

ASOKA: What are you babbling about?

JAILER: The royal edict stating that no man is ever to leave
                    this prison alive.

ASOKA: Hmmm, aren't you a sly one . . . but still not a king. *(He beckons to someone offstage.)* Guard, take out the holy man and put this jailer in his place! At once!

Scene V: Royal palace, that evening.

AIDE: The Buddhist teacher has arrived.

ASOKA: Bring him in.

(Enter BOYA.)

BOYA: You seek to know more of the Buddhist way?

ASOKA: Yes, indeed. Today, I witnessed something incomprehensible. A man of your beliefs was in great physical pain, yet his face was serene. Never have I seen such inner peace.

BOYA: That is our ultimate goal . . . inner peace.

ASOKA: But how do you attain it?

BOYA: Selfishness is the root of all life's woes and troubles. The Eightfold Path, as taught by the Buddha, can stamp selfishness out.

ASOKA: Is the Path hard to follow? How do I know if I'm on it?

BOYA: When we earnestly seek only good, and the well-being of others, the Path becomes clear.

ASOKA: The well-being . . . even of our enemies?

BOYA: The secret of life is love. The crowning jewel of the Buddhist way is love for one's enemies.

ASOKA: Tell me more. Tell me more.

Scene VI: Royal palace, days later.

AIDE: Yes, my King.

ASOKA: Bring me my vizier.

(Enter VIZIER.)

I have become a Buddhist, and wish to spread the message of Buddhism far and wide. There will be great changes throughout the Empire.

VIZIER: I await your commands.

ASOKA: Demolish the royal dungeon. No more torture. Inform all my officials that I want my subjects to feel as if they're my children. I want them treated with only great patience and fairness.

VIZIER: Those are significant changes.

ASOKA: I want my people educated and inspired to lead more fulfilling lives. But how can I communicate my thoughts and feelings to all of them? The Empire is so vast.

VIZIER: What thoughts and feelings in particular?

ASOKA: That all religions must be peacefully tolerated. That we should all strive to be kind and pure in deed, truthful in word, and merciful in judgment.

VIZIER: You have indeed changed! These are most noble and lofty sentiments . . . . Why not write them on signs and place them throughout the Empire?

ASOKA: That's it! I'll use the local dialects . . . my new edicts will appear on rocks and pillars for all to see.

VIZIER: Anything else?

ASOKA: Buddhist monasteries for teaching and meditation. We must build thousands of them. More hospitals. Sanctuaries to protect animals. Replace the royal spies with "officers of virtue" to teach goodness and encourage peace throughout the whole realm. Plant more fruit trees. Expand the irrigation system to help the poorer farmers . . . .

AIDE: Oh, King. Your commanding general has arrived.

(Enter FAYNG.)

FAYNG: Your troops have won a great victory over the Kalinga rebels. Thousands of the traitors are dead. Many more are now prisoners.

ASOKA: How tragic! They are my children, too. Free the prisoners. Restore the Kalingas to their tribal lands. Send an official letter to their leaders expressing my great sorrow over their sufferings and losses.

FAYNG: My King . . . I . . . I don't understand.

ASOKA: I want no more of war! Enough of mindless slaughter and destruction. From this day on the only troops I'll send out will be missionaries of the Buddhist way: people of peace, truth, love, and gentleness.

Ancient China: The Ch'in and
Han Dynasties, 221-87 B.C.

```
┌─────────────────────────────────────────────────────────────────┐
│                          Characters                                │
│                                                                    │
│   LOI and SAN,                      HAN and HUANG,                 │
│     Chinese peasants                  Chinese intellectuals        │
│   FO, an aide to the emperor        WU-TI, Han emperor             │
│   CHENG (Shih Huang-ti),            SZUMA, an aide to Wu-ti        │
│     first Chinese emperor                                          │
│   LI, chief minister to                                            │
│     Shih Huang-ti                                                  │
└─────────────────────────────────────────────────────────────────┘
```

Scene I: State of Ch'i, China, 221 B.C.

LOI: Old friend, have you heard the news?

SAN: From the battlefront? No. What's the latest?

LOI: It's over . . . the forces of Ch'in have triumphed.

SAN: How tragic! Now what can we expect? I've heard our new masters are especially brutal.

LOI: They're no different than the other warring states, except the Ch'in are more efficient.

SAN: You didn't answer my question. How will our lives be different?

LOI: I'm no sage, but I'm told their leaders are driven by two forces—

SAN: Greed and power, like all conquerors.

LOI: Of course . . . but for a higher purpose: to unify all the great separate states into one great China.

SAN:	After today, it appears they've succeeded. But how will they rule us?
LOI:	According to the second force which drives them: the Legalist philosophy.
SAN:	Which is?
LOI:	A society based on countless laws, all very specific, all strictly and impartially enforced.
SAN:	And who makes these laws?
LOI:	The ruler. All power rests with him and his court.
SAN:	What about the old local ruling families?
LOI:	Their power and influence will surely decline.
SAN:	It sounds as if great changes are in store for all our people.
LOI:	Yes, but I'm certain it will take some time and great effort by our new leaders.

Scene II: Hsien-yang, China, 221 B.C.

FO:	Master . . . Ch'i is defeated. All the warring states are now under your power.
CHENG:	Yes, but not my dominion. Now the important work begins, building a new political and economic order.
LI:	Where should we start?
CHENG:	With the feudal lords and regional chieftains. Their power must be crushed and obliterated!
LI:	That won't be easy.

CHENG:	But it must be done! What caused all the disunity and discord of the Chou? The feudal system! I will completely abolish it! No more hereditary provincial governors.
LI:	Then who will govern in their place?
CHENG:	My people! All of the new China will be organized into thirty-six provinces, each with a governor and military leader.
LI:	But how will you keep the civilian governor from getting too powerful in his province? He'll be a long way from your capital.
CHENG:	Simple. I'll continually rotate them among the thirty-six different provinces so they won't have time to build a power base.
LI:	And when friction arises between the civilian and military leaders, how will there be peace?
CHENG:	Through a third official . . . who will strike a balance between the two.
LI:	And how else will you tie the country together?
CHENG:	Through the equal enforcement of all laws.
LI:	How about business and commerce, your new economic order?
CHENG:	Comprehensive standardization of our weights and measures. For example, every wagon axle length should be the same.
LI:	Very wise. Every new road will share the same width. That will be more efficient.
CHENG:	Of course. Speaking of roads, we must construct many, many more.

LI: So you can quickly send your troops to trouble spots.

CHENG: Yes, and move farm products more easily. Also, we must build more canals to nurture our agriculture. Remember, I want to break the stranglehold of the feudal lords.

LI: And the peasants?

CHENG: Give ownership of the land to them.

LI: Any changes in the money system?

CHENG: Yes. We will standardize the currency throughout the realm. Any new ideas from you?

LI: I'm working on a simpler writing script that should expand literacy.

CHENG: Excellent! Oh, I forgot something. My official title will be "Shih Huang-ti."

LI: "First Sovereign Emperor." Yes, but your title and changes will not sit well with the old feudal powers. You can't realistically expect your local representatives to control them.

CHENG: Very perceptive. But I have a solution. They'll all be required to live here, in my capital, where I can keep an eye on them.

LI: Brilliant! Your enemies will be contained like snakes in a jar.

CHENG: Not all of them. Have you forgotten the barbarians to the west and north?

LI: Invite them to join the feudal lords living here.

CHENG: Li, you're an amusing wit. We could keep them out with one great wall.

LI: Possibly, but it would have to be fifteen hundred miles long! The cost would be staggering.

CHENG:	Of course, but it must be done. Don't forget—parts of the Great Wall are already in place. We'll keep costs down by using lawbreakers for most of the labor.

Scene III: Hsien-yang (capital), China, 213 B.C.

FO:	Emperor, unrest grows throughout the country.
CHENG:	People resist change, even when it benefits them later.
FO:	They complain about the taxes and laws.
CHENG:	Of course they do. They see only a small picture, painted for today. My vision is for all China, today and tomorrow. In time they'll lose affection for the old ways.
FO:	Many are very determined to return to the old days.
CHENG:	Absurd! Those were the times of poetry, but not peace; art, but not order. Let's round up these agitators and nudge their feet closer to the fire. Who are they, anyway?
LI:	Many of them come from the learned classes.
CHENG:	Oh . . . the same fluff-heads who waste their time reading literature and discussing philosophy? Why don't they realize only agriculture and the military are worthwhile?
LI:	They are very stubborn, and their influence is growing. We're at a crisis point. What will you do?
CHENG:	Silence all criticism and complaining! Write up a new law.
LI:	But how do you silence ideas?
CHENG:	A fish dies when denied water. A new decree: "All books not concerned with science, agriculture, or Ch'in laws and history must be burned! Forced labor for all violators." Let the pointy heads finally do something useful: work on the Great Wall.

24 Exciting Plays for Ancient History Classes

LI:	Very wise. Anything else?
CHENG:	I need to travel more throughout the entire country . . . in secret, so I can see if our laws and policies are really being followed.

Scene IV: Ch'ang-an (Han capital), 175 B.C.

HAN:	Huang, do you ever think about the old days?
HUANG:	Yes. There were police everywhere, and our precious books were burned.
HAN:	And punishment, even for trivial offenses, meant mutilation.
HUANG:	Those were dark and mean times before the Han triumphed.
HAN:	Yes, indeed. Remember how we kept the light of Confucius burning by memorizing the books?
HUANG:	We each took a text, so all of them would be remembered.
HAN:	Life is so different under our new emperor. We have freedom of speech and writing.
HUANG:	We can even criticize the government! What great burdens have been lifted from the people.
HAN:	Yes . . . the harsh laws and high taxes.
HUANG:	And the emperor seeks peace. How different from before.
HAN:	It's almost amusing. Instead of the sword, this emperor offers his enemies great gifts!
HUANG:	Like the Yin and the Yang, the frozen winter has passed . . . .
HAN:	And an ocean of flowers blooms . . . .

Scene V: Lo-yang (Han capital),
140 B.C.

WU-TI: Because you're an historian, I want you to record my philosophy, and my goals for the kingdom.

SZUMA: Very good, Emperor.

WU-TI: All government officials are to be men of the highest character, virtue, and learning. Family connections and wealth *must not* count for selection. Furthermore, these officials are not to govern through fear or by bribery.

SZUMA: You mean the selection exams are to be open to all, regardless of background?

WU-TI: Precisely. And advancement will be based upon merit.

SZUMA: Confucius would be pleased!

WU-TI: Scholarship and the arts must be encouraged and promoted throughout the country.

SZUMA: Economic matters?

WU-TI: All natural resources are to be owned and operated by the government.

SZUMA: Like the salt and iron industries?

WU-TI: Especially them. Prices, especially for food, must be stable . . . and reasonable.

SZUMA: How can you do that? Aren't you dreaming?

WU-TI: No. We must eliminate the middleman's excessive profits.

SZUMA: Please explain.

WU-TI: If we create a state monopoly in the transport and distribution of food—

SZUMA: You'll do away with the middleman's price markups.

WU-TI: Exactly.

SZUMA: But that won't stop the speculators.

WU-TI: Controlling the supply will. When there is a crop surplus the government will buy that surplus and store it to keep prices from falling.

SZUMA: And thereby save the peasant farmers from ruin.

WU-TI: Yes. And during shortages the government will release the surplus food to keep prices down and discourage hoarding.

SZUMA: What enlightened ideas . . . .

WU-TI: And to further insure fairness, we'll expand the currency by adding tin to the silver.

SZUMA: More money in circulation will certainly benefit the little person.

WU-TI: For the unemployed we'll sponsor public works projects like roads, bridges, and canals.

SZUMA: And how will you finance them?

WU-TI: All incomes will be registered with the government. Each person will pay a five percent tax.

SZUMA: Very ambitious. Your foreign policy?

WU-TI: Push back the barbarians! Extend Chinese rule to Korea, Manchuria, Turkestan, and Indo-China.

SZUMA: Will you have enough time for all this?

WU-TI: I hope to rule for a half century.

Cleopatra, Queen of Egypt

```
┌─────────────────────────────────────────────────────────────┐
│                          Characters                            │
│  POTHINUS, a court official      APPOLODORUS,                 │
│  ACHILLAS, an Egyptian              Cleopatra's aide          │
│     general                      CAESAR, Roman military       │
│  CLEOPATRA, Egyptian                leader                    │
│     queen                        FLATUS, an aide to Caesar    │
└─────────────────────────────────────────────────────────────┘
```

Scene I: Royal palace, Alexandria, Egypt, 51 B.C.

POTHINUS: Achillas, our time has come. Auletes, Ptolemy XI, is dead.

ACHILLAS: Good riddance! I'm surprised the degenerate old goat lived so long. Do you think Egypt now faces another royal succession crisis?

POTHINUS: For our purposes, I hope so.

ACHILLAS: What do you mean, Pothinus?

POTHINUS: Custom dictates that Cleopatra, being the king's oldest child, should rule.

ACHILLAS: Anything wrong with that? We can certainly work our desires through a vain and empty-headed teenaged girl.

POTHINUS: Not so. You greatly underestimate Cleopatra's independent spirit and keen intelligence. My spies tell me she has secretly surrounded herself with four brilliant teachers. We must mine our political hopes in more fertile ground.

ACHILLAS: Her ten-year-old brother?

POTHINUS: Yes. We can easily control him.

ACHILLAS:	But what about Cleopatra? Her people will now move quickly to consolidate power in her name.
POTHINUS:	Of course they will. But we'll immediately begin steps to undermine her authority . . . we'll spread rumors and gossip about her personal life. We'll sow the seeds of suspicion and jealousy in the palace so that more drastic measures will be accepted as just.
ACHILLAS:	Yes . . . and then our time will come.

Scene II: Royal palace, 49 B.C.

CLEOPATRA:	Appolodorus, friend and adviser, what am I to do?
APPOLODORUS:	My Queen, what do you mean? You have reigned wisely and well. The people adore you.
CLEOPATRA:	But my enemies sow intrigue everywhere. They're constantly trying to discredit me with lies.
APPOLODORUS:	You mean Pothinus and Achillas. Go after them!
CLEOPATRA:	I can't. They control most of the palace. My own food taster died today! I don't feel safe here.
APPOLODORUS:	Then you must leave! There is more to Egypt than Alexandria. Go to the desert and win the loyalty and support of the tribal chiefs. Bide your time safely there until the situation changes.
CLEOPATRA:	You are right, Josephus has taught me to speak the language of the desert. Now I can use that training.
APPOLODORUS:	That will surely win the chiefs' hearts!
CLEOPATRA:	I hope so. But I'll need more than their support. No Egyptian ruler is beyond mighty Rome's shadow.

APPOLODORUS:	A most unfortunate price for our disunity.
CLEOPATRA:	Still, I will not grovel before the Romans like my weak and dissolute father did. I want Egypt to regain her independence and self-respect.
APPOLODORUS:	So do I. But you still need Roman support to deal with your enemies here.
CLEOPATRA:	I know. But whose favor do we seek? Who now rules Rome?
APPOLODORUS:	At present the issue is in doubt. Rome is undergoing great political changes. My sources inform me that their republican form of government will soon end. The Senate is losing power.
CLEOPATRA:	What form of government will replace the Senate?
APPOLODORUS:	A single strong leader. Already two men are struggling for dominance—Caesar and Pompey.
CLEOPATRA:	Then we must be careful to link our fortunes with the victor.
APPOLODORUS:	When will you leave the palace?
CLEOPATRA:	Tonight. During the play I will excuse myself because of a headache. Have a fast boat ready.

Scene III: Desert region, Egypt, 48 B.C.

APPOLODORUS:	My Queen, you grow more beautiful each day.
CLEOPATRA:	Cut the false flattery. You know me better.
APPOLODORUS:	I mean what I say. For a year and a half you have lived the rugged life of a desert warrior, and it has deepened your beauty. Besides, don't the people adore you?

CLEOPATRA:	Here, yes. But in the capital I'm branded a fugitive. Each day I'm away from the palace I lose more of my power and authority to Pothinus and Achillas.
APPOLODORUS:	Don't be so pessimistic. Interesting news about Rome's power struggle has arrived from the East. Caesar has emerged the victor.
CLEOPATRA:	And Pompey's fate?
APPOLODORUS:	He sought refuge in Pelesium. When he landed, Pothinus immediately had him killed, hoping, I guess, to win Caesar's favor.
CLEOPATRA:	A foolish act, but an opening for us.
APPOLODORUS:	I don't understand.
CLEOPATRA:	Romans are driven by a sense of honor, even regarding their rivals and enemies. Caesar would despise an Egyptian for treating another Roman the way Pothinus did. Where is Caesar now?
APPOLODORUS:	Sailing for Alexandria to settle Egypt's turmoil.
CLEOPATRA:	Then I must get to him immediately.
APPOLODORUS:	Too dangerous. Achillas's men are everywhere. Once you're spotted they'll kill you.
CLEOPATRA:	I'll take the risk. Can you get me into Alexandria?
APPOLODORUS:	Maybe, but not into the palace.
CLEOPATRA:	Just get me to Saat. He'll know what to do.

Scene IV: Royal palace compound, Alexandria, a short time later.

CAESAR:	Flatus, answer the door.

24 Exciting Plays for Ancient History Classes

FLATUS:	Yes, Caesar.
CAESAR:	Well . . . what or who is it? I'm very tired after working so long on this juvenile and idiotic Egyptian political mess.

(Enter RES, carrying a Persian carpet.)

FLATUS:	A gift from a respected palace official named Saat.

(RES unrolls the carpet, revealing CLEOPATRA.)

CAESAR:	Who are you? Flatus, inform this servant that I don't need some dirty and foul-smelling wench to warm my bed. You Egyptians have no class.
CLEOPATRA:	Class? Ha! You Romans shamelessly prance like peacocks after trampling women and children under your soldiers' heavy feet.
CAESAR:	Guards! Remove this deranged Egyptian alley cat.
CLEOPATRA:	You think your many legions give you license to make the whole world Roman subjects?
CAESAR:	And why not? The world outside Rome is in chaos. We intend to bring it order and stability.
CLEOPATRA:	Slaves live stable and orderly lives . . . as long as they obey their masters.
CAESAR:	For an Alexandrian alley cat you have a quick mind.
CLEOPATRA:	And a love for Egypt!
CAESAR:	Who are you, anyway?
CLEOPATRA:	Cleopatra, daughter of Ptolemy XI, and rightful queen of Egypt.

CAESAR:	Ridiculous! You expect me to believe you after the way you derided Rome? Some way to win my friendship and influence my actions on your behalf, young lady!
CLEOPATRA:	Forgive me, I was only defending Egypt's honor.
CAESAR:	A noble gesture, then. But tell me . . . since when do Egyptian queens dress like ragged farmers and smell like dockworkers?
CLEOPATRA:	I have come from the desert, where I have been hiding. I have been fighting against the treacherous forces of Pothinus and Achillas.
CAESAR:	The men behind your brother, Ptolemy XII?
CLEOPATRA:	Yes. They claim that only he is the rightful ruler. But I have my father's will to disprove them—I am to rule jointly with my brother.
CAESAR:	Show it to me.

(She gives it to him.)

CLEOPATRA:	Now do you believe me?
CAESAR:	I do.
CLEOPATRA:	Then arrest the traitors!
CAESAR:	Ha! One moment you degrade Roman power, and the next, you wish to use it. You're not a cat, but a fox.
CLEOPATRA:	Again, great Caesar, forgive me. I really know little about you Romans.
CAESAR:	Very well, then. I'll teach you. Above all, we Romans are practical people. We want results. Whatever means work to those ends, we use.

CLEOPATRA:	The heavy hand and pointed spear.
CAESAR:	Is that always practical? No. We use force only when absolutely necessary. We do not believe in squandering our forces or political goodwill.
CLEOPATRA:	Then what's your solution for Egypt?
CAESAR:	Reconciliation. Tomorrow we'll have a banquet bringing together all contending forces. My plan is to have that feast, not force, resolve Egypt's ruling crisis.
CLEOPATRA:	Thank you, Caesar.
CAESAR:	Now run along and clean yourself up!
CLEOPATRA:	I can't. If I leave your protection I'll be killed.
CAESAR:	Then we'll just have to bring your bath and clothes here. Guards, see to our guest while I'm planning tomorrow's affair.

Scene V: Banquet hall, royal palace, the next day.

FLATUS:	Caesar! It's a trap! Run for your life!
CAESAR:	Don't worry. I was prepared for this. My spies just executed Pothinus before I arrived. Arrest Achillas and the boy-king.
FLATUS:	I'm afraid they've both escaped . . . in all the confusion.
CAESAR:	It looks as if we're in a very messy situation.
CLEOPATRA:	And a very dangerous one, too, especially if Achillas controls all the ships now docked.
CAESAR:	Let me see a map of the city. With Achillas's forces here, and the ships able to move there, we'll be trapped in a pincers. We can't let Achillas use those ships!

CLEOPATRA: Caesar, where are you going?

CAESAR: To the harbor to burn those ships! Appolodorus, show us the fastest way there!

Scene VI: Royal palace, later that evening.

CAESAR: Cleopatra . . . Cleopatra! Get a hold of yourself. Why all the weeping? Rejoice! The revolt is crushed. Achillas and your brother are dead.

CLEOPATRA: What have you done?

CAESAR: What do you mean, what have I done? I've risked my very life to preserve your crown. Isn't that what you desired?

APPOLODORUS: My Queen, be grateful. Caesar nearly drowned while setting fire to the ships.

CLEOPATRA: Come to the window and see the Romans' handiwork.

APPOLODORUS: The royal museum and library are in flames!

CLEOPATRA: The greatest library in the world will soon be nothing but bitter ashes.

CAESAR: Do you think my men did that intentionally? The winds spread the fires from the ships to the warehouses and then to—

CLEOPATRA: The library and museum were my homes!

CAESAR: Cleopatra! At this very moment my men are risking their lives to save every possible book and artifact.

CLEOPATRA: You don't understand what this loss means to Egypt.

CAESAR: I think I do, and also what the civil war has cost your country. Rome will not abandon you during your recovery.

CLEOPATRA:	Great Caesar, stay here in Egypt and help me. I will do everything in my power to make your time pleasant and productive.
CAESAR:	Your beautiful voice gives me great pleasure, but I can't stay too long. Duty beats a loud drum in Rome.
CLEOPATRA:	Just stay long enough to help me consolidate my authority in all of Egypt. Come with me as I inspect my realm. We'll cruise together up the Nile.
CAESAR:	A wise ruler knows first-hand the problems and concerns of his subjects. Your offer tempts me.
CLEOPATRA:	*Her* subjects . . . then it's finalized. You will stay in Egypt.

New Testament Times: The Parable of the Good Samaritan

<table>
<tr><td colspan="2">Characters</td></tr>
<tr><td>PUAH, REZON, and
  ZEKE, lawyers
DAN, a traveler
CALEB, a friend of Dan
SLUHG and BAASH, robbers
PRIEST</td><td>LEVITE, a lay religious official
DARIS, a Samaritan
EBAL, an innkeeper</td></tr>
</table>

Scene I: Outside a synagogue, Judea, c. A.D. 28.

PUAH: Rezon, how goes the great legal scholar and wit?

REZON: Fair . . . I've just had an encounter with that Jesus of Nazareth.

ZEKE: The carpenter's son? The one the desperate classes claim has miraculously fed thousands, and cured the sick and handicapped?

REZON: The same one.

PUAH: I've heard he tells interesting stories.

REZON: Very . . . they sneak up on you.

PUAH: What do you mean? Surely someone with your brains and experience would never be caught off guard by the words of a mere carpenter's son.

REZON: Do you two know anything about boxing?

PUAH: I've seen some off-duty Roman soldiers box.

ZEKE: Me, too. I guess the Greeks taught them.

REZON: Then you know a boxer defends against either a right-hand or left-hand blow.

PUAH: Well . . . of course. Even an idiot or a Samaritan knows as much.

ZEKE: What are you getting at? What happened between you and this Jesus?

REZON: I went after him, securely confident I could expose his ignorance and shallow thinking. I was going to humiliate him to the core.

ZEKE: You've verbally knocked out every scholar and intellectual around here. What happened this time?

REZON: It was like being hit by an unseen hand.

PUAH: I see no bruises . . . did he humiliate you?

REZON: No. That doesn't seem to be his nature or style, though I'm certain he knew I was trying to trap him.

PUAH: What did you ask him?

REZON: How a person could inherit eternal life.

ZEKE: His response?

REZON: He calmly asked me what the Law said.

PUAH: Certainly no man around here knows the Sacred Law better than you. What did you say?

REZON: The standard: Love the Lord your God with all your heart, soul, strength, and mind. Love your neighbor as yourself.

ZEKE: Pretty smart of him to have you answer your own question. Was that the end of it?

REZON: No, no. That's when I really thought I had him.

PUAH: How? What else could you ask?

REZON: Who my neighbor was.

ZEKE: Hardly a question for a decisive war of wits.

REZON: Wrong. I saw it becoming a canyon he could not cross. I saw him falling deeper and deeper into—

PUAH: What do you mean?

REZON: If he answered specifically, I could counter back with "Why not so and so? Isn't he my neighbor, too?"

ZEKE: And you're sharp enough to pepper him endlessly with more possibilities—

PUAH: Until you forced him to conclude, "Everyone is my neighbor."

REZON: Which would be a meaningless generalization, a linguistic contradiction, and a graphic proof of shallow thinking.

ZEKE: And he would have been publicly humiliated.

PUAH: Well, how did he answer "Who is my neighbor?"

REZON: He told this story . . . .

Scene II: A street in Jerusalem.

DAN: Well, good friend, I'm off for Jericho.

CALEB: Be careful. There are snakes everywhere along that road. You need a traveling companion.

DAN: I'll carry a stick . . . don't worry about me.

CALEB: I'm not talking about serpents! Robber vipers are all along
                   that route, especially those scum Samaritans.

DAN: I'll be fine. It's a busy road, so if I have any problems I'm
                   sure many will come to my aid.

Scene III: On the road
from Jerusalem to Jericho.

SLUHG: Here comes an easy mark.

BAASH: Looks well dressed, too. He should have a fat purse.

SLUHG: A perfect setup for us . . . no one within shouting distance.
                   I'll get his attention from the front . . .

BAASH: While I belt him hard from the rear. Should we completely
                   take him out?

SLUHG: Yeah . . . it's better that way. Then you don't have to worry
                   about them coming after you.

BAASH: Right . . . I like to see them bleed and beg. Let's go.

                   (Enter DAN.)

SLUHG: Hello, stranger. Any water to spare?

DAN: Certainly . . . I have some right—

                   (BAASH strikes him. DAN is then severely beaten.)

BAASH: Somebody's coming. Let's get out of here.

                   (Enter a PRIEST.)

PRIEST: What's that lying over there on the ground? Oh, my . . . another tragic statistic. Nothing I can do here, so I might as well hurry on . . . .

(Enter a LEVITE.)

DAN: Help . . . help.

LEVITE: Oh . . . another innocent victim of mindless violence. Poor man. He looks near death. I'd better not let him see me. I'm sure he only wants me to put him out of his misery. I . . . I . . . I'm not capable of that. I'll just move to the other side of the road. But I'll be sure to inform the authorities on ahead . . . .

(Enter DARIS, a Samaritan.)

DAN: Help . . . please, someone help me.

DARIS: Oh, how terrible! Here, take some water, please. Be strong. I'm not going to let you die! This is going to hurt, but I must clean your wounds. There, there. Hold still now. I'm going to put you on my donkey, and get you some help.

Scene IV: Inn along the road, hours later.

EBAL: Oh my gosh! What happened to your companion?

DARIS: Robbers attacked him and left him for dead.

EBAL: Let me take a look. Oh, those are nasty cuts and bruises . . . . Say . . . he's . . . he's not a Samaritan like you.

DARIS: I'm a Samaritan, it's true. I don't know who or what he is, except a man in great need.

EBAL: What gives? His people and your people only come together to hate.

DARIS: An evil that can and should be ended.

EBAL: No chance, dreamer! But tell me, why would you, a Samaritan, bother to help this man? His people have despised your people and treated them like dirt for generations.

DARIS: I must go in the morning. I'm going to leave this man in your care until I return. Take these coins and spare no expense in seeing to his recovery. If they aren't enough, I'll reimburse you fully when I return.

EBAL: I may be a hard-headed innkeeper, but at least I'm an honest one. These coins should be more than enough. But I still don't understand why you're doing this. This man is a stranger.

Scene V: Return to Scene I setting.

ZEKE: Then what happened?

REZON: Jesus asked which of the three—the priest, the Levite, or the Samaritan—was a neighbor to the robbed and beaten man.

PUAH: And how did the great lawyer respond?

REZON: I said, "The one who showed mercy and kindness."

ZEKE: It seems this Jesus more than bridged your philosophical canyon.

PUAH: Did he say anything else?

REZON: Yes, and with great authority. He told me to go and live like that Samaritan.

Rome, A.D. 67

Scene: Mamertime dungeon, Rome, Italy, A.D. 67

JAILER:	All right, you dungheads! Move quickly! Into the cell . . . I said move it!
SERVIUS:	Bite your tongue, chain-brain. Show some respect to a war veteran.
JAILER:	You'll get the respect of raw meat, swine! Now move quickly, or you'll taste the lash.
SERVIUS:	Go ahead! You can't hurt me. I've battled from here to Britain and back . . . all for our glorious Empire. Never met any kitten cowards like you.
JAILER:	Oh, yeah? Tell me if this feels like a kitty's tail. Take that! *(Lashes him with whip.)*
SERVIUS:	Aren't you tough? Hitting a guy whose hands are chained. You suck sewer water, mutton-mug.
JAILER:	Oh, aren't we funny. Here's more of the lash!
LUCIUS:	Enough! How dare you! The man's a citizen!
JAILER:	What are you babbling about, flabface?

LUCIUS: The rights of a Roman citizen under the law. Rome isn't a barbarian German forest.

JAILER: Shut up, all of you! Just move into the cell. There's a lot more scum coming.

MARIUS: Try treating us with some dignity.

JAILER: So the smiling dog can speak. I'll treat you as I wish! I'm in charge here!

MARIUS: Are you, now? Your whip is, and it does a poor job of getting us to obey.

JAILER: It's all I have to help me do this lousy job.

MARIUS: There are weapons of the spirit . . . love, patience, understanding . . . .

JAILER: I see your drift. Convicts . . .

SERVIUS: Prisoners, you mean. We have not been convicted of any crimes yet.

JAILER: Fine. *Prisoners* accused of treason against imperial—

LUCIUS: Wait! Try "prisoners of conscience."

JAILER: *(sarcastically)* Prisoners of conscience, please accompany me to your holding cell.

SERVIUS: Now you're on a real Roman road. Come on, now. Follow me, double time!

JAILER: Finally . . . be seated . . . please.

(JAILER exits and locks door.)

LUCIUS: What has happened to Rome? Maybe we *are* in a barbarian-infested forest.

SERVIUS:	It's not the Rome I left for the army many years ago.
LUCIUS:	I agree. Things have definitely changed for the worse. Why are you here? Troubles with your commanding officer?
SERVIUS:	Not at all. I always got along . . . because I went along.
LUCIUS:	Meaning?
SERVIUS:	Like all loyal Roman soldiers, I did what I was told. Things turned sour when I came home.
LUCIUS:	Oh? How's that?
SERVIUS:	Before my army days I was a farmer. After my discharge I discovered that my family had been kicked off the land while I was away.
MARIUS:	What! How could that be?
SERVIUS:	Simple. Some of the local land hogs and their patrician cronies put the big tax squeeze on. With me gone, there was no one to fight them.
LUCIUS:	And then? What happened to your family?
SERVIUS:	Eviction. They came here to Rome for jobs. I found them in the workers' slum district.
MARIUS:	How terrible! And you who spent so many years in army service. What appreciation.
SERVIUS:	I'm not alone. So many have lost their farms to the greedy rich. You know . . . to the ones with the political connections.
LUCIUS:	I know, I know. I once belonged to that class.
MARIUS:	Let him tell his story.

SERVIUS:	Well . . . I, too, came to Rome looking for work. When I saw the hordes living in dirty slums and eating the rotten bread the government handed out, I decided to act. That's the soldier in me.
LUCIUS:	What did you do?
SERVIUS:	I started organizing people like myself who had lost their land. I was arrested while leading a large group to the Forum.
LUCIUS:	What happened at your trial?
SERVIUS:	Trial? I had no trial. The authorities were afraid to give me one.
MARIUS:	Because you are a veteran, a loyal citizen, and a Roman seeking justice.
SERVIUS:	Precisely. The ruling classes fear open rebellion.
MARIUS:	And well they should. That's why they sponsor all these gory games and circuses . . . to distract the people and diffuse our dangerous energies.
SERVIUS:	Of course. If the suffering masses think, they'll organize and rebel . . . and our so-called law-and-order society will crumble.
LUCIUS:	I believe the crumbling began long ago.
SERVIUS:	You think so? Say, you mentioned belonging to the patrician class. Why are you here?
LUCIUS:	Treason, like everyone else these days.
MARIUS:	Patricians aren't like everyone else. You must have done something extreme to offend the authorities.
LUCIUS:	You have it backwards.
MARIUS:	I don't understand.

LUCIUS:	The authorities have done the offending, not me. I simply told a crowd at the Forum how Rome had lost her way.
SERVIUS:	I'm still confused.
LUCIUS:	Do you think Rome was always governed like this? Our emperor Nero is both mad and barbaric. How many people has he tortured and put to death? He's even had his own wife and mother killed.
SERVIUS:	You spoke publicly against the emperor?
LUCIUS:	Yes, and against his most recent predecessors, too. Remember Claudius? His harlots and secretaries were deciding the Empire's fate. And that madman Caligula before him . . .
MARIUS:	The same Caligula who made his horse a consul?
LUCIUS:	Yes, and caused a terrible stir in Palestine by putting up his own statue in a Hebrew temple.
SERVIUS:	You spoke of all these things?
LUCIUS:	I did . . . to alert Rome to its spreading rot.
SERVIUS:	And what did the authorities do?
LUCIUS:	They took me aside and said my brain was going soft and my memory foggy. They lectured me on Rome's greatness: her buildings, roads, aqueducts, and sanitation systems. They went on and on, glorifying our literature, drama, and legal system.
SERVIUS:	And your response?
LUCIUS:	I agreed, and acknowledged all these great achievements. But I said they would fade and die if the corruption rotting our civilization was not checked.

MARIUS:	They arrested you just for saying that?
LUCIUS:	No. After they released me I returned to the Forum and publicly called for a return to the republic. That was too much to ignore, even from a patrician. So here I am. We must bring back justice and the rule of law, as in the past.
SERVIUS:	Agreed. And we'd better clean up the army while we're at it. The officers are all greedy and the troops are disloyal and unreliable. Hannibal would have easy pickings today.
	(Enter JAILER with a badly beaten man.)
JAILER:	Here's some more company for you . . . a religious rabble-rouser. Excuse me . . . another prisoner of conscience.
MARIUS:	Paul! What have they done to you? Jailer, please bring some clean water and a cloth.
JAILER:	I'll see what I can do. *(Exits.)*
SERVIUS:	They sure did a job on him. What a beating! Do you think he'll live?
MARIUS:	Yes. He's a man of great endurance.
LUCIUS:	Paul? Is he that famous preacher of the Nazarene sect?
MARIUS:	Of the Christian faith. Paul is our leader here in Rome.
SERVIUS:	Didn't the emperor Nero blame you Christians for Rome's great fire?
MARIUS:	Yes. We were greatly persecuted. Many of us went underground.
LUCIUS:	Tell us about Paul. I've heard he's converted many to this new religion, especially slaves and the poor.

24 Exciting Plays for Ancient History Classes

MARIUS:	He was originally named Saul. He was born in Tarsus of a very religious and learned Hebrew family. When the new religion began spreading from Jerusalem, Saul actually persecuted the Christians.
SERVIUS:	How?
MARIUS:	He would bring Christians before religious courts to be hassled. Once he even guarded the coats of those who stoned Stephen, our first martyr, to death.
LUCIUS:	And this same man preaches the Christian religion today? How can this possibly be?
MARIUS:	After Stephen's death, Saul journeyed to Damascus. There, he intended to root out still more Christians. Along the way he fell suddenly to the ground, blinded, he said, by a great light.
SERVIUS:	How did this change him?
MARIUS:	Once blinded, he said a voice called to him, asking why he was persecuting the Christians. Paul said it was the voice of Jesus, the One we believe is the Christ.
LUCIUS:	Then what happened?
MARIUS:	Since he couldn't see, Paul's traveling companions had to guide him to Damascus. There, a man named Ananias anointed him, and his sight was restored.
SERVIUS:	Who was Ananias?
MARIUS:	A Christian. He had had a vision foretelling his encounter with a man named Saul. In this vision he saw that Saul would become a great missionary to the Gentiles.
LUCIUS:	Wasn't Ananias afraid of Saul?
MARIUS:	He certainly was. All the Christians knew of Saul's malicious reputation. But Ananias obeyed his vision.

SERVIUS: And did Saul, or Paul, as you now call him, fulfill that promise?

MARIUS: Indeed! Paul, more than any single person, spread the Gospel of Jesus Christ beyond Jerusalem to Asia Minor, Greece, Macedonia, and Rome itself.

LUCIUS: You said Paul was a man of great endurance. In what ways?

MARIUS: So many. He has walked over a great part of the Roman Empire, discoursed with Greek intellectuals for hours, been beaten, left for dead, jailed, shipwrecked, and even bitten by a snake. He's very persistent.

SERVIUS: Like a good Roman soldier.

LUCIUS: And why are you a follower of this new religion? It could cost you your life.

SERVIUS: Seeing Christians fight wild animals in the arena is a popular spectacle these days.

MARIUS: I will not deny my faith. If the emperor judges loyalty to my faith as treason, I plead guilty.

SERVIUS: And that means death. But you still have not answered Lucius's question. Why do you follow this new way?

MARIUS: Look at the official religion of Rome. It's not a religion of love, but lust. It stands for power, not peace. It's a religion of greed, not grace . . . of classes in conflict, not community . . . of fighting, not forgiveness.

LUCIUS: Well said. And your religion teaches differently?

MARIUS: Yes, the opposite of the state religion. We look to Jesus of Nazareth as our model and hope of salvation.

SERVIUS: Tell me more about your hope. People like me don't have much these days.

LUCIUS: I think this Christian religion will prove attractive to many.

MARIUS: Our Lord told us to preach the Gospel to the ends of the earth.

SERVIUS: The Empire's great system of roads will certainly make that goal easier.

24 Exciting Plays for Ancient History Classes

Christianity and the Roman Empire,
A.D. 177-323

Characters

FLATUS, an imperial aide
AURELIUS, an emperor
BRUTUS, a citizen
SORDIS, a citizen
CALLAS, an imperial official
ATTALUS, a Christian leader
BLANDINA, a Christian
GUARDS
CONSTANTINE, a future
  emperor

HELENA, Constantine's
  mother
GALERIUS, a high imperial
  official
DIOCLETIAN, an emperor
LYDIA, Galerius's wife
LACTANTIUS, Constantine's
  aide
LICINIUS, an imperial
  military leader

Scene I: Imperial court, Rome, A.D. 177.

FLATUS:	Emperor, I have an urgent message from Lyons! There is growing unrest and violence against the Christians.
AURELIUS:	Whether it's famine or flood, plague or war, unemployment or high prices, the ignorant masses blame the Christians.
FLATUS:	For good reason. The Christians refuse to pay homage and respect to the Roman gods.
AURELIUS:	Well . . . what does the imperial legate in Lyons want?
FLATUS:	Clarification of the laws and punishments regarding adherents of the Christian religion.
AURELIUS:	I see. Officially, we've been rather lenient toward them.
FLATUS:	Unless the officials regain their enforcement authority, the masses will take the law upon themselves . . . and do more than just throw stones at the Christians.

AURELIUS:	Of course. If one law isn't respected, all laws are in jeopardy. What's been done so far?
FLATUS:	Over fifty Christians have been jailed, including their bishop, Pothinus . . . who died in his cell.
AURELIUS:	Of natural causes?
FLATUS:	The effects of legal procedures . . . besides, he was ninety. Your decision regarding the others?
AURELIUS:	Freedom for those who renounce Christianity. Death, according to the law, for those who persist.
FLATUS:	And the particular means of enforcement?
AURELIUS:	I'll leave that up to the legate's discretion.

Scene II: Amphitheater, Lyons, Gaul, A.D. 177.

BRUTUS:	The festival games have never been more entertaining!
SORDIS:	I've heard the best is yet to come.
BRUTUS:	Some new races?
SORDIS:	No. A little drama and a little sport, starring the Christians. *(laughs)* . . . if you know what I mean.
	(Enter CALLAS, ATTALUS, BLANDINA, and GUARDS.)
CALLAS:	Attalus, if you publicly recant the Christian religion, you will be freed.
ATTALUS:	I will never deny my Lord and Savior.
CALLAS:	Guards, unveil the chair.
BRUTUS:	What's that strange color?

24 Exciting Plays for Ancient History Classes

SORDIS:	The glow from red-hot iron. I'd say the Christian's on the hot seat now! *(He laughs.)*
CALLAS:	Blandina, Attalus was a leader of the Christian community. You are only a slave girl. You need not share his fate. Only renounce Christianity. Others have, and then they were sent home.
BLANDINA:	I belong to Christ. I have no home without Him.
CALLAS:	Guards! Tie her and put her in the bag.
BLANDINA:	May Christ bless and forgive you all.
	(GUARDS place BLANDINA in bag.)
BRUTUS:	Look! A bull is loose in the arena.
SORDIS:	It's headed straight for the bag!
BRUTUS:	Look at the size of his horns!
SORDIS:	Hey, I like this . . . that bull just tossed the girl halfway across the arena! But I don't think she'll last long.
BRUTUS:	*(laughing)* A little longer than her well-done friend.

Scene III: Moesia (Bulgaria), A.D. 280.

CONSTANTINE:	Mother, why don't you honor the Roman gods?
HELENA:	Because I'm a Christian.
CONSTANTINE:	Why? Nobody likes them.
HELENA:	My son, you are still a boy, but old enough to understand some hard truths. Your father may be a high official in the Roman Empire . . .

CONSTANTINE: Some day he'll be emperor.

HELENA: But do you know what I was before he met me? A barmaid. My people come from the lowest and poorest class. When we were sick and hungry, do you think the selfish Roman officials cared? No! But the Christians cared for us, and fed us.

CONSTANTINE: But you don't have to worry about such problems now.

HELENA: My son, I am only your father's concubine. Besides, not all the wealth and power of Rome could have changed my cousin as our Savior did.

CONSTANTINE: What do you mean?

HELENA: My cousin was a very bad man. He lied, cheated, and used everyone, even his family, for his own selfish desires. Christians changed him.

CONSTANTINE: Was he tortured?

HELENA: Only his spirit. No, he was not tortured as many Christians have been. When he saw how bravely many of them faced death, he went to the Christian community.

CONSTANTINE: And? What happened?

HELENA: They knew of his bad reputation, but welcomed him in Christian love. In time he was changed. He became kind, honest, and loving. No pagan god of the mighty Empire could have done that! Never forget that as you become a man and leader.

Scene IV: Imperial court, Nicomedia, A.D. 303.

GALERIUS: Emperor, the fate of the Empire is at stake. Unity must be restored, regardless of cost.

DIOCLETIAN: Who could doubt that? But you can't buy unity with gold or simply decree it from the throne.

GALERIUS: True, but you can rally the populace by destroying once and for all the parasite Christians.

DIOCLETIAN: How? They're growing in number and influence. Others have tried eliminating them, and failed.

GALERIUS: They weren't systematic enough.

DIOCLETIAN: Meaning?

GALERIUS: Destroy all their churches and books. Dissolve their congregations and confiscate their properties. Punish by death those who publicly assemble.

DIOCLETIAN: Oh, all right. Draw up the necessary orders and distribute them at once.

Scene V: Imperial court, Nicomedia, A.D. *311*.

GALERIUS: All is lost. Civil war, again! Maximinus and his son Maxentius against Constantine and Licinius. The Empire is torn and tattered like a cheap tunic.

LYDIA: Husband, you are very ill. Before it's too late, make your peace with my God. You have seen He cannot be defeated.

GALERIUS: You are right. Persecution seems only to strengthen them. I will issue an edict recognizing Christianity as a lawful religion.

LYDIA: And . . .

GALERIUS: Ask Christians for their prayers.

24 Exciting Plays for Ancient History Classes

Scene VI: Constantine's camp, near Rome, October 26-27, A.D. 312.

CONSTANTINE: How go the battle preparations?

LACTANTIUS: Maxentius is trapped. His back is against the Tiber. He has no means of retreat except over the Milvian Bridge. Brilliant strategy, Constantine.

CONSTANTINE: Thank you. I don't think Maxentius expected us to cross the Alps so quickly. I'll see you at dawn.

Scene VII: The next morning.

LACTANTIUS: You have an unusual look in your eye, Constantine.

CONSTANTINE: Yesterday, when I was alone, I had a vision—a flaming cross and the words *In hoc signo vinces.*

LACTANTIUS: "In this sign you shall conquer."

CONSTANTINE: And in my sleep a voice commanded my soldiers to mark on their shields an *X*, with a line drawn through it that curls around the top.

LACTANTIUS: Why, that's the symbol of Christ. Will you so command the troops?

CONSTANTINE: Yes! And my standard will bear the initials of Christ interwoven with a cross.

LACTANTIUS: Don't worry about the troops' reaction to this order. Many are already Christians.

CONSTANTINE: Good. Send out the command, and ready the troops for battle.

(Exit, then enter again shortly.)

LACTANTIUS: Victory! Maxentius and thousands of his troops lie dead in the Tiber. Constantine, you are master of the West!

Scene VIII: Milan, Italy, early A.D. 313.

LICINIUS: Constantine, it looks as if you've finished your work in the West. I still have Maximinus to deal with in the East.

CONSTANTINE: We both have lots of work ahead, and not with our swords.

LICINIUS: We always have administration problems.

CONSTANTINE: True. But we can greatly ease our burdens by confirming Galerius's edict for religious toleration.

LICINIUS: And extend it to all religions in the Empire?

CONSTANTINE: Yes. And restore all property seized from the Christians. Both measures will generate much needed support for our reigns.

Scene IX: Imperial court, Rome, A.D. 315.

LACTANTIUS: Terrible news from the East. Licinius is persecuting the Christians all over his domain.

CONSTANTINE: That snake! I suppose he fancies himself the emperor of all pagans, and me the emperor of the Christians. We'll have a reckoning, and the Empire will no longer be divided.

LACTANTIUS: It's best to strike a snake only when it's distracted.

CONSTANTINE: Wise counsel. We must be patient.

Scene X: Constantine's camp, Scutari, A.D. 323.

LACTANTIUS: Message from Licinius. He will surrender all his forces, but only if you promise him a pardon.

CONSTANTINE: So be it. There's been enough bloodshed.

LACTANTIUS: But he's still a snake, and dangerous.

CONSTANTINE: No. He lost his fangs at Adrianople, and now he's shed his skin at Scutari.

LACTANTIUS: Yes . . . you are sole emperor. What are your new dreams?

CONSTANTINE: To bring unity, peace, and harmony to the whole Empire again.

LACTANTIUS: Then will you decree Christianity the new state religion?

CONSTANTINE: I will support freedom of worship for all . . . and invite my subjects to join me in following the Christian faith.

The Fall of the Roman Empire in the West

Characters

FLATUS, an imperial aide	**TREV**, a Visigoth
CONSTANTINE, an emperor	**SICCHO**, an imperial aide
SKEPTUS, an imperial aide	**VALENS**, an emperor
THADUS, a Roman military aide	**DOMUS**, a Roman soldier
SLEEG, a Roman general	**WESTUS**, a Roman baker
FRITIGERN, a Visigoth leader	**REGOR**, a Visigoth
	ALARIC, Visigoth king

Scene I: Byzantium, November, A.D. 324.

FLATUS: Emperor, we can barely keep up with your pace. How far will you go in tracing the boundaries of the new capital?

CONSTANTINE: Till the Lord Almighty stops me. *Nova Roma* shall be the grandest and most handsome city in the world. We will build the largest churches, widest streets, most beautiful parks, and biggest amphitheater.

SKEPTUS: Why not rebuild the old Rome?

CONSTANTINE: The future of the Empire lies here in the East.

FLATUS: You've chosen an ideal location for trade and commerce. It's truly the crossroads of the world.

CONSTANTINE: And ideally suited for defense: rushing waters on three sides.

SKEPTUS: And the old Rome? What shall be its fate when the capital is moved here to Byzantium?

CONSTANTINE: The fate it deserves.

Scene II: Roman army outpost, Danube River, A.D. 377.

THADUS: General, Visigoths are entering the area. Their leader wishes to speak with you.

SLEEG: What are their numbers? Can we hold them back? Do they want tribute?

THADUS: No. This group is in no condition to extort money. They may be remnants of a recently slaughtered Goth army.

SLEEG: Oh? Slaughtered by whom? Bring me their leader.

(Enter FRITIGERN.)

FRITIGERN: General, my people have suffered greatly. Our homes and farms are destroyed. I ask you, I beg you, allow us to cross the river and settle peacefully in Moesia and Thrace.

SLEEG: Who caused all this death and destruction?

FRITIGERN: Huns from the East. They are like a great and mighty flood that cannot be dammed.

SLEEG: What do you mean?

FRITIGERN: My people fight to live. The Huns live to fight. In war they never stop, not for pain, rest, water, or food. They ride swift horses as easily as we walk. Their leaders are cunning as foxes and resourceful as beavers.

SLEEG: Your people may stay here until I receive instructions from Emperor Valens. But you must expect terms for your protection.

Scene III: Visigoths' camp, across Danube, months later.

TREV: Fritigern, the situation in the camp worsens. We've paid too great a cost for safe passage.

FRITIGERN: Have those greedy and cynical Roman officials again raised food prices?

TREV: Beyond our honor. Demanding all our silver was bad enough. Now they seek to trade food for our innocent boys and girls.

FRITIGERN: Those debauched Romans! What are the parents doing? Surely, they are not giving in to those shameless pigs.

TREV: When hunger hunts honor, terrible things happen. Those near starvation are selling their children. They're given no other choice.

FRITIGERN: And they call *us* barbarians! We, who are hospitable and honest, even to strangers. We who honor chastity and punish adultery.

TREV: You were wise to refuse to surrender our weapons.

FRITIGERN: We have lost everything but our honor and good sense. Those virtues we will never give up! Alert the men. It's time the Roman perverts paid our price.

Scene IV: Roman outpost, Danube River, soon after.

THADUS: General, the Visigoths grow increasingly restless. Our informers predict that open rebellion will soon break out.

SLEEG: Ungrateful barbarians! I'll soon put a stop to that. Invite their leader to a banquet here tonight.

THADUS: What are your plans?

SLEEG: We'll stuff that trousers-wearing, long-haired pig and feed him to our dogs! That will drench any spark left in that scum.

Scene V: Emperor's court, Constantinople, A.D. 378.

SICCHO: Emperor! The Goths are rampaging all over Thrace!

VALENS:	What? Didn't they give up their arms for safe passage across the Danube?
SICCHO:	They were supposed to, but corrupt officials there were bribed.
VALENS:	Wasn't the Goth leader assassinated?
SICCHO:	A trap was set, but he cleverly escaped.
VALENS:	Assemble the forces. We must move quickly to exterminate these barbarian vermin, or their cleverness will prove our undoing.

Scene VI: Battlefield, plains of Hadrianople, days later.

FRITIGERN:	Is the battle over?
TREV:	Almost. Our cavalry routed the Roman infantry. Two thirds of their army perished. Their emperor and his aides have taken refuge in a nearby cottage. Your orders?
FRITIGERN:	Burn it!

Scene VII: Marketplace, Rome, A.D. 410.

DOMUS:	Westus, my friend, no bread for sale today?
WESTUS:	Not a loaf. I can't buy any flour!
DOMUS:	How can that possibly be? You've been a baker in the city for over twenty years. You must know every supplier in Rome.
WESTUS:	I do, but they all give me the same angry answer: There's very little grain being harvested anymore.
DOMUS:	That's ridiculous. People haven't stopped eating.

WESTUS:	Of course not. But thousands of once-productive farms are now deserted. The high taxes have ruined the small farmers. The old economic system is near collapse.
DOMUS:	What are you going to do?
WESTUS:	Leave. Rome is rotting. Where are the people? The rich throw parties behind their walled villas in the countryside. Merchants can't be found because they can't buy stock. Nobody works anymore. Every other day is some holiday, and the people are off to some silly show or bloody contest.
DOMUS:	It's just as bad in the army. Our own citizens refuse to serve anymore. Do you realize that most of the troops defending Rome are barbarians? Stilicho was a Vandal!
WESTUS:	True, but he saved us from Alaric and his Goths.
DOMUS:	And how did the emperor reward our noble German protectors? Death. Death because of jealousy and intrigue at the imperial court. Hundreds besides Stilicho were slaughtered!
WESTUS:	What is the military situation facing Rome now?
DOMUS:	Very grave. Alaric has amassed a huge and formidable army—many of his soldiers are from Stilicho's forces. Even worse, many Huns have joined him.
WESTUS:	Will Alaric attack?
DOMUS:	Not unless he's provoked. He and his Goths are very disciplined. My greatest fear is the Huns.

Scene VIII: Alaric's camp, outside Rome, A.D. 410.

REGOR:	The Roman Senate has put to death the widow of Stilicho.
ALARIC:	What shameless cowards! And they brand us as barbarians?
REGOR:	Then shall we attack the city?

24 Exciting Plays for Ancient History Classes

ALARIC:	No. We'll block all roads in and out of Rome. When they begin to starve, we'll ask for terms: all their movable wealth.

Scene IX: Alaric's camp, days later.

REGOR:	A delegation from the city has arrived.
ALARIC:	Their response to my offer?
REGOR:	A definite no. They complain that the terms are too harsh, that they are left with nothing.
ALARIC:	Nonsense . . . I'm leaving them with their lives.
REGOR:	They warn that a million Romans will fight us.
ALARIC:	Is that so? And what do they say about the thousands of their slaves who will surely join our side? They're bluffing. These soft-muscled and smooth-skinned Romans won't fight. Long ago they abandoned any causes they'd die for.

Scene X: Alaric's camp, days later.

REGOR:	The terms have been accepted.
ALARIC:	Very well. Open the roads.

Scene XI: Alaric's camp, days later.

REGOR:	Alaric! Sarus has deserted to the Roman side.
ALARIC:	How many troops did he take with him?
REGOR:	Many. They've started attacking our main army.
ALARIC:	I wonder how much those conniving Romans paid him.
REGOR:	Your orders?

ALARIC:	Destroy Sarus! Take the city, but spare all the churches and those who take sanctuary in them.

Scene XII: Inside Rome, three days later.

REGOR:	Commander! The Huns and former Roman slaves have gone wild! Everywhere they're slaughtering, raping, stealing, and destroying.
ALARIC:	Get my most loyal and disciplined regiment . . . immediately! We must restore order, else all will be lost.
REGOR:	Very well. Do you think Rome is finished?
ALARIC:	The old Rome certainly is. Only the crumbtakers and curious who follow us will keep this rotten corpse from a final burial.